KAMEN NEVENKIN

THE TANK BATTLES OF MARSHAL ROKOSSOVSKY

AN ILLUSTRATED STUDY OF THE MOST IMPORTANT OPERATIONS OF CENTRAL, 1ST BYELORUSSIAN AND 2ND BYELORUSSIAN FRONTS,

1943 - 1945

PUBLISHED BY
PeKo Publishing Kft.
8360 Keszthely, Bessenyei György utca 37.
Email: info@pekobooks.com
www.pekobooks.com

RESPONSIBLE PUBLISHER
Péter Kocsis

AUTHOR
Kamen Nevenkin

EDITOR
Tom Cockle

LAYOUT
Adam Nagy / nadam.hu

PRINTED IN HUNGARY

FIRST PUBLISHED
2021

ISBN 978-615-5583-66-7

TABLE OF CONTENTS

CHAPTER 1

THE MAKING OF THE COMMANDER

EARLY LIFE AND CAREER

Konstanty Rokossowski was born on 21 December 1896[1] in Warsaw, then part of the Russian Empire, to a Polish father and a Russian mother. His father, Ksawery Wojciech Rokossowski, a railway inspector, descended from a noble family of cavalry officers. His mother, Antonina Ovsyannikova, was a school teacher from the Pinsk area (in today's Byelorussia). He was baptized Orthodox Christian, but it is quite probable that later on was raised a catholic.

Konstanty was left an orphan at age of 14 and was forced to earn his living by working in a stocking factory. In the next year he became an apprentice stonemason. He also attended high school but never graduated.

At the outbreak of the World War I, Rokossowski volunteered in the 5th "Kargopol" Dragoon Regiment. Upon enlistment his name (Konstanty) was Russified to Konstantin, which would be easier to pronounce. Given the fact that since early age he was an avid reader of history and was very much fascinated by the great ancient commanders, it is possible that the decision of the young Rokossowski to join the army was fueled to a considerable degree by naivety and military romanticism.

Right from the outset the 5th "Kargopol" Dragoon Regiment was involved in bitter battles against the Germans, first in the central sectors of the Eastern Front, and later on in Latvia. Rokossowski distinguished himself already during the opening clashes. In the summer of 1915 he was awarded Cross of St. George 4th Class, his first ever military decoration. He got two more St. George Crosses (3rd and 2nd Class, respectively), during the following two years. In the meantime he gradually rose in ranks and in the spring of 1917, upon attending an NCO course, was promoted to sergeant.

1 His birthday was disputed by the Russian historian Boris Sokolov, the author of Marshal's most recent biography. Sokolov claims that Rokossovsky was most likely born in 1894.

* * *

Rokossowski joined the Bolshevik Party in 1917 and by the end of the same year entered the ranks of the rapidly growing Red Army. By then he also had completely Russified his patronymic and family name to (Konstantin) Konstantinovich Rokossovsky.

The personal file of Konstantin Rokossovsky in the Russian Military Archive (TsAMO) clearly sets his nationality as being Polish. However, it is not very clear whether the future Marshal of the Soviet Union had ever considered himself a true Pole or pretended to be a Russian. Most probably, he forever remained some kind of foreign body to both Poles and Soviets. It is difficult to say whether Rokossovsky was a fanatical Bolshevik, but there is no doubt that he remained faithful to communist ideals for the rest of his life.

The still very young Red Army suffered from a critical shortage of well-schooled men and especially of officers. Not surprisingly, the battle-hardened high-school undergraduate was considered well educated (compared to the mass of semi-literate peasants) and almost immediately appointed to command a cavalry squadron. During the Russian Civil War he led his men in several fierce engagements with the White Guard in the Urals where he was wounded (in the shoulder) in late 1919.

Rokossovsky quickly rose in ranks and in 1921 he was already in charge of a whole cavalry regiment. The service to the new regime brought him to places like China and Mongolia, where he for the first time was able to show his qualities as a military commander. (In Outer Mongolia, in particular, he defeated the forces of the mystic Baron von Ungern-Sternberg, a Rasputin-like figure who reportedly believed he was the reincarnation of Genghis Khan.) It was in Mongolia where Rokossovsky met his wife, Julia Barmina, a high-school teacher and a very-well educated lady who was fluent in four languages and who had thoroughly studied Greek mythology. The couple married in 1923 and two years later they welcomed a baby girl, Ariadna, who would be their only child.

In 1924-1925 Rokossovsky attended the Higher Cavalry School in Leningrad, where he first met Georgy Zhukov. Their paths would cross many times over the following decades. Then he returned to the Far East, where he spent the next several years.

Marshal Rokossovsky with his wife Julia Barmina (right) and daughter Ariadna shortly after war's end. (RinP)

Initially, he was a trainer for the Mongolian Communist armed forces, serving in this capacity for a period of two years (till July 1928). From January to April 1929 Rokossovsky attended an advanced staff course in the Frunze Military Academy in Moscow where he became familiar with the works of Mikhail Tukhachevsky. Then the future Marshal of the Soviet Union was transferred to the Special Red Banner Eastern Army under Vasily Blyukher. While serving there, he took part in yet another conflict, the Russo-Chinese War of 1929–1930 (the so-called Eastern Railroad War), as commander of the 5th Independent "Kuban" Cavalry Brigade.

Upon his return from the Far East Rokossovsky's career skyrocketed. In January 1930 he was put in command of the 7th "Samara" Cavalry Division. (One of the brigades of that division was led by Georgy Zhukov.) In February 1932 he was transferred again, this time to 15th Independent Cavalry Division, where he held simultaneously the positions of divisional commander and commissar. In 1935 Rokossovsky finally was promoted to general's rank (*Komdiv*[2]). The following year he was appointed commander of the 5th Cavalry Corps, which was quartered in Pskov.

Rokossovsky was among the first to recognize the full potential the armored fighting vehicles. He was fascinated by Tukhachevsky's theory of deep operations in which combined arms formations strike deep behind enemy lines to destroy the rear services and logistics.[3] He was not alone in his views. Given how influential the cavalry branch in the Red Army was at the time, it seemed that nothing could stop the young and obviously gifted Soviet general from reaching the heights of a military career. He was ambitious, in good shape and fully devoted to his job. His future seemed bright. And then disaster struck.

* * *

In August 1937 Rokossovsky became caught up in the Great Purge unleashed by Stalin, arrested and accused of being a spy. It is possible that his arrest had something to do with his adherence to Tukhachevsky's theories, which were bitterly opposed by some conservative senior Red Army officers such as Semyon Budenny, who still favored traditional cavalry warfare. The fact that the young corps' commander was associated with the Special Red Banner Eastern Army of Marshal Blyukher (who was arrested shortly afterwards) must be taken into consideration, too. His Polish roots also had played a part - he was accused not only of spying for Japan but also of delivering secret information to the Poles.

During the interrogations Rokossovsky was severely beaten by the NKVD thugs, but despite the torture he refused to sign a false statement. This most likely saved his life and after the trial he was sent to the Kresty Prison in Leningrad. But even there he refused to acknowledge Stalin's chief role in the purges and remained a blind follower of Communist ideology. Even the fact that his imprisonment affected the lives of his immediate family (his wife and daughter were sent to external exile, where they struggled to make ends meet) didn't change his mind.

2 *Komdiv* is the abbreviation to Commanding officer of the Division. It was a military rank in the Red Army from 1935 to 1940 and was a Major-General equivalent.

3 K. Rokossovsky, "Soldatsky Dolg", Moscow, Veche, 2013, p. 5.

A Soviet armored column rolls through a countryside during the bloodless annexation of Bessarabia in the summer of 1940. The most powerful vehicle, a T-26 tank, leads the column followed by several BA-10 armored cars outfitted with 45-mm guns. (WA)

* * *

On 22 March 1940 Rokossovsky was released from the Kresty without explanation. Following a period of some recuperation in Sochi, the main Russian sea-side resort, where he was joined by his family, he returned to active service. (He was appointed back as the commander of the 5th Cavalry Corps at the rank of Colonel.) His restoration to active duty had a lot to do with the efforts of the new People's Commissar for Defense of the Soviet Union, Semyon Timoshenko, who desperately sought ways to modernize and expand the Red Army after the fiasco in the Winter War with Finland. There was an urgent demand for experienced and open-minded officers to fill command posts and Rokossovsky was considered one of them.

In June-July 1940 the 5th Cavalry Corps participated in the occupation of Bessarabia, which proved to be Rokossovsky's last mission as cavalry officer. Soon he was promoted to the rank of a Major-General (the return of some traditional Tsarist Army officer ranks was also part of Timoshenko's reform) and put in charge of forming the 9th Mechanized Corps in the Kiev Military District.

* * *

The 9th Mechanized Corps was established in December 1940. Initially it consisted of the 19th and 20th Tank Divisions, and the 131st Motorized Infantry Division. In February 1941 the 19th Tank Division was replaced by the 35th Tank Division, but this didn't improve the overall combat value of the corps, because its units were critically short of all types of materiel and the personnel were very much undertrained. Worse still, the 35th Division existed only on paper and had to be raised from scratch.

By the outbreak of the war the corps was deployed in the Western Ukraine, in the vicinity of Novograd-Volynsky, northeast of Zhitomir. Despite the repeated drills and active training, its military worth increased very little, because the quantities of equipment and materiel arriving from the factories and stores were insufficient. Apart from that, most of the manpower consisted of green recruits, while military professionals were scarce. Thus, the 20th Tank Division was short almost 75% of its required NCOs, and about 50% of its officers and technicians. The 35th Tank Division fared no better – even though it had received most of its enlisted men, only 60% of the required NCOs and about 30% of the officers were on hand.

Equipment shortages were appalling. The 131st Motorized Division had only 664 motor vehicles of all types on hand (out of the authorized 1,400). The rifle regiment of the 35th Tank Division was completely on foot, and there were only 7 tractors in the entire formation, which made its howitzer regiment virtually immobile. The 20th Tank Division, which was supposed to be Rokossovsky's main striking formation, was the least equipped. It had less than 40 tanks, let alone that because of the lack of vehicles most of its equipment and heavy weapons could not be moved, while the men would go into action on foot. Undoubtedly, the biggest problem of the corps was that it didn't receive any modern tanks, namely the fearsome T-34s and KVs.

STRENGTH OF THE 9TH MECHANIZED CORPS,
1 June 1941

20th Tank Division: 30 BT tanks, 3 T-26 tanks, 3 OT-26 flamethrower tanks, 28 artillery pieces, 4 AA guns, 244 motor vehicles, 38 tractors, 10 motorcycles
35th Tank Division: 141 T-26 tanks, 1 OT-26 flamethrower tank, 10 artillery pieces, 4 AA guns, 188 motor vehicles, 7 tractors
131st Motorized Division: 104 T-26 tanks, 18 amphibious tanks, 40 artillery pieces, 4 AA guns, 595 motor vehicles, 69 tractors, 17 motorcycles

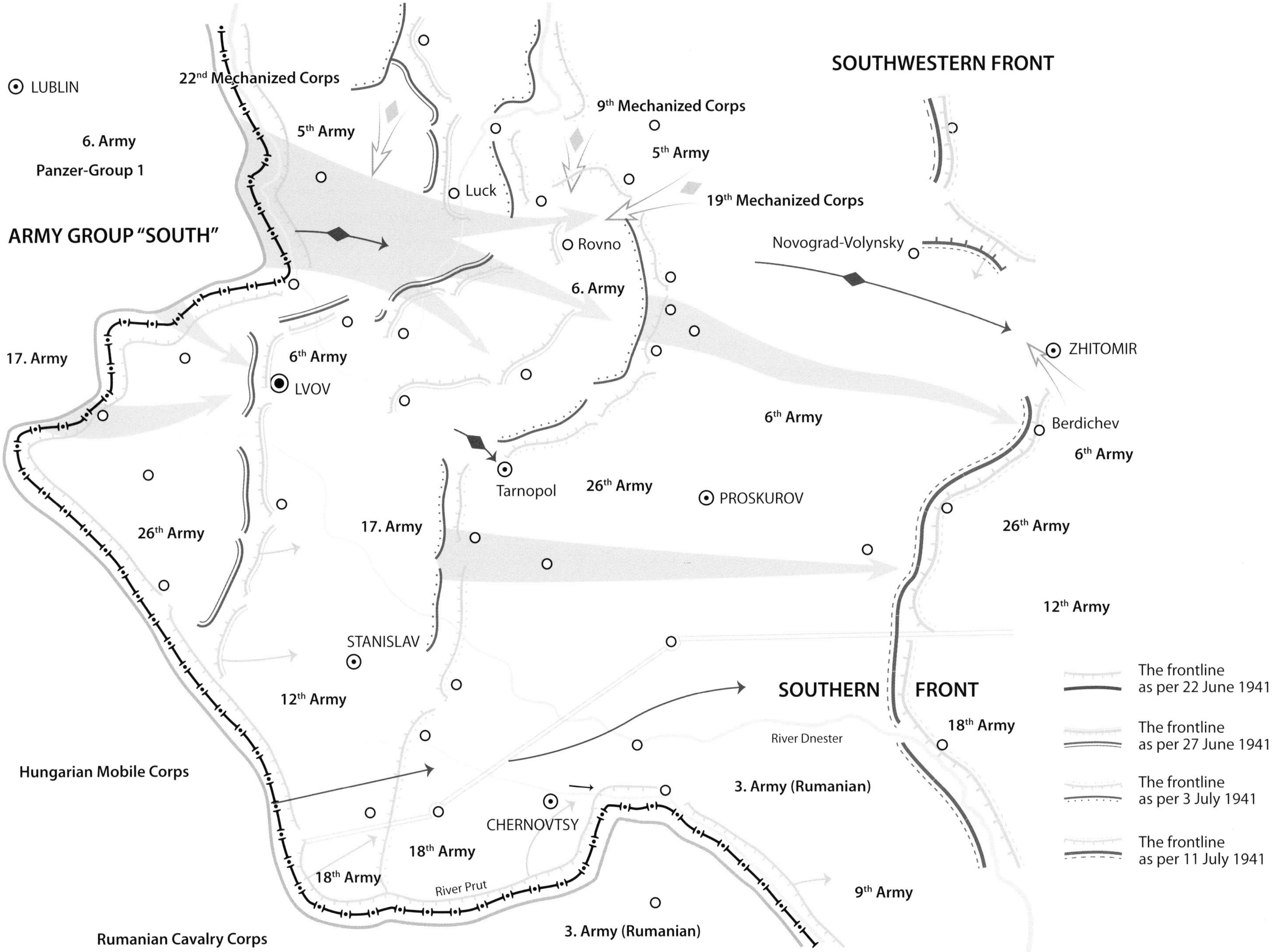
SOUTHWESTERN FRONT
LUBLIN
22nd Mechanized Corps
9th Mechanized Corps
6. Army
Panzer-Group 1
5th Army
5th Army
Luck
19th Mechanized Corps
ARMY GROUP "SOUTH"
Rovno
Novograd-Volynsky
6. Army
17. Army
6th Army
ZHITOMIR
LVOV
6th Army
Berdichev
6th Army
Tarnopol
26th Army
PROSKUROV
26th Army
26th Army
17. Army
12th Army
STANISLAV
SOUTHERN FRONT
12th Army
18th Army
River Dnester
Hungarian Mobile Corps
3. Army (Rumanian)
CHERNOVTSY
18th Army
18th Army
River Prut
9th Army
Rumanian Cavalry Corps
3. Army (Rumanian)
The frontline as per 22 June 1941
The frontline as per 27 June 1941
The frontline as per 3 July 1941
The frontline as per 11 July 1941

THE WAR BEGINS: THE TANK BATTLE OF BRODY

Nazi Germany invaded the Soviet Union on 22 June 1941. Three powerful army groups, designated "North", "Center" and "South", delivered powerful blows in the directions of Leningrad, Moscow and Kiev, respectively.

In the Ukraine the main blow was delivered by Panzer-Group 1 of *Generaloberst* von Kleist, who was under orders to seize the crossings over the Bug River, then advance on Rovno with the ultimate objective of capturing Kiev. It was made of five panzer divisions with less than 730 tanks between them, of which about 450 were outfitted with guns (3.7 cm or above). On the other hand, all five divisions were balanced formations made up not only of tanks, but also of infantry, artillery, engineers, tank-killers, all of them fully motorized. Their mobility was guaranteed by the large number of trucks (up to 2,000 per division) available to each of them. Most importantly, all five divisions (or their elements) already had passed the test of battle, completely proving their combat worth in Poland, Western Europe and in the Balkans.

Against them General Mikhail Kirponos, the commander of the Southwestern Front, threw a real armada – six mechanized corps totaling more than 3,400 tanks, of which nearly 700 were the newest Soviet models, T-34/76, KV-1 and KV-2. The result was the largest tank battle in the history of warfare, involving more than 3,000 machines (not all Soviet machines reached the battlefield, mainly due to mechanical breakdowns.)

A German infantryman carrying a Karabiner 98k rifle stares at a fallen Soviet tanker somewhere in the Western Ukraine, June 1941. A knocked-out Soviet BT-7 Model 1935 tank of an undisclosed unit is burning in the background. (RA)

Apparently, General Kirponos possessed an overwhelming superiority over the enemy, but this was only on paper. The actual condition of the other five corps was not much different from the one led by Rokossovsky. Especially troubling for their commanders was the severe shortage of vehicles, which meant the infantry and artillery could not accompany the tanks, while the lack of maps and communication/signal equipment promised very poor coordination. Worse still, the mechanized formations were hindered by lack of fuel and spare parts, and were pretty much defenseless against the constant Luftwaffe aerial attacks. (While all German tanks were provided with radios since the late 1930s, the Soviet commanders still had to rely on signal flags to change the directions of the movements of their armored units.)

Yet another problem was the absence of any previous combat experience. Proper terrain reconnaissance was not carried out; the vehicles, the columns and the positions were not adequately camouflaged.

AFV STRENGTH OF 11., 13. AND 14. PANZER-DIVISIONS,
22 June 1941

11. Panzer-Division: 44 Pz II, 24 Pz III (3.7 cm), 47 Pz III (5 cm), 20 Pz IV, 8 PzBef
13. Panzer-Division: 45 Pz II, 27 Pz III (3.7 cm), 44 Pz III (5 cm), 20 Pz IV, 13 PzBef
14. Panzer-Division: 45 Pz II, 15 Pz III (3.7 cm), 56 Pz III (5 cm), 20 Pz IV, 11 PzBef

* * *

The 9th Mechanized Corps entered the battle on 24 June in the vicinity of Lutsk. The march to the front was carried out in the most difficult conditions: communication breakdowns, repeated strafing attacks of the Luftwaffe, shortage of motor vehicles, masses of panicked refugees and friendly troops retreating in disarray. Needless to say, all this considerably delayed the arrival of the divisions at their assembly points.

Unlike most of his counterparts, during those chaotic days Rokossovsky displayed his best qualities as a commander and officer. Right from the very first days of "Barbarossa" he showed a great deal of initiative and courage. Without any sanctions from his superiors, he ordered the military stores and warehouses in the vicinity to be opened by force. His troops seized about 200 trucks, plus considerable quantities of ammunition and supplies. Rokossovsky also refused to obey some senseless orders, for instance, when he was ordered to launch "suicide" counterattacks.

The corps operated against the northern shoulder of the German armored "wedge" where von Kleist had committed to battle 13. and 14. Panzer-Divisions. The clashes between the 13th Panzer and 9th Mechanized were fierce. For instance, already during the first engagement the 20th Tank Division lost many of its tanks. But the Germans also sustained bloody losses. The report of one of the battalions of Panzer-Regiment 4 (13. Panzer-Division) shows that between 24 and 28 June the number of operational machines had dropped from 65 to 31.

By the end of 26 June Rokossovsky was finally able to assemble all his forces for a counterattack. While the troops were gathering in the assembly area, the corps commander observed with dismay a large number of Soviet soldiers of various decimated units wandering through the woods. He immediately ordered his staff officers to round them up and incorporate them into the corps' formations.

On the morning of 27 June the 9th Mechanized Corps at last was able to deliver a powerful counterattack. The divisions of Rokossovsky crushed the northern flank of 13. Panzer-Division and succeeded in cutting off for awhile its rear communications. But then the Germans recuperated and managed to restore the situation. Having found gaps in the Soviet flanks, they threatened the corps with encirclement and forced it to withdraw.

On 28 June Rokossovsky's units, together with several other badly mauled formations of the 5th Army, fought tooth and nail to prevent Rovno being captured by the Germans. Despite the fanatical resistance put up by them, by nightfall the Soviets abandoned the town. The corps, nevertheless, remained in possession of the vital position north of the Lutsk – Rovno road and by doing so kept threatening the northern flank of Kleist's panzer group.

The attempts of the Southwestern Front to parry the German advance by mobile defense methods didn't go unnoticed by the German High Command. *Generaloberst* Franz Halder, the Chief of the General Staff, wrote in his diary:

> AG South is advancing slowly, unfortunately with considerable losses. The enemy on this front has energetic leadership. He is continuously throwing new forces against the tank wedge, attacking frontally, as before, and now also the southern flank, and . . . the northern flank.[4]

Reconnaissance troops of SS-Leibstandarte Adolf Hitler riding a Zündapp military motorcycle with sidecar move through a destroyed settlement, Ukraine, July 1941. The soldier wearing a cap is presumably armed with a Karabiner 98k rifle. The motorcycle in front of them carries two Model 1924 Stielhandgranate hand grenades. (NAC)

4 A. Harding Ganz, "Ghost Division", Mechanicsburg, Stackpole Books, 2016.

Troops of the Reconnaissance Battalion of SS-Leibstandarte Adolf Hitler in action during the opening days of Operation Barbarossa, Western Ukraine, July 1941. The infantrymen wear camouflage smocks and helmet covers, a hallmark of the Waffen SS personnel until the end of the war. Most of them are obviously armed with Karabiner 98k rifles, while the machinegun crew operates an MG 34. The Leibstandarte insignia is clearly visible on the Sd.Kfz. 222 armored car. (NAC)

On 1 July the 9th Mechanized Corps delivered its last full-scale counterattack. The action performed by the 20th Tank Division proved to be especially successful. The units of Colonel Mikhail Katukov, a future renowned tank army commander, hit hard the flank of the German 25. (Motorized) Infantry Division and even encircled some of its elements northwest of Rovno. The disaster was avoided thanks to the timely arrival of SS-Division *"Leibstandarte SS Adolf Hitler"*. As usual, the first who appeared on the battlefield were the men of the reconnaissance battalion. On their way to Rovno they most likely had some clashes with the vanguards of the 9th Mechanized. On the next day the elite SS division struck the positions of Rokossovsky's left-hand neighbor and pushed it to the northeast. Kurt Meyer, the commander of the LSSAH Reconnaissance Battalion, vividly recalls the first action of his unit on the Eastern Front:

> A couple of kilometers east of Luck, next to a railway line, we came across the last outposts of an infantry battalion. Dense smoke clouds showed us the location of a destroyed Russian tank. Dark forests were on either side of the road along which we were moving eastwards. We had to hurdle a distance of sixty kilometers to reach Rowno. Would we reach our objective in time and would we be able to give our comrades of the 25. Infanterie-Division (mot.) tangible assistance? Calmly, I gave the lead elements the signal to start the move into the coming night. In the lead was Fritz Montag. Montag was a veteran of the First World War and was the platoon leader of a motorcycle platoon in the l./ SS-Aufklarungs-Abteilung 1.
>
> At first slowly, then more swiftly, the spearhead moved towards the dark forests. I wanted to shout out: "Stop! What I preached to you isn't true! The engine isn't your friend. Move slowly, or you will drive to your death!" But my lips wouldn't open. They were pressed together to protect themselves from the air stream. Squinting my eyes, I followed the lead elements of the column boring further and further into the forest.
>
> Destroyed Russian tanks were on both sides of the road. Trucks and horse drawn vehicles were abandoned beneath the trees. At one place, we found twelve camouflaged Russian T-26s. They were without fuel, deserted. Ready for combat, the battalion moved past a large area of heath that extended north. Suddenly, I saw the lead platoon disappear in front of me and the 20 mm cannon of an armored car fire at some bushes. Four or five of these "bushes" then moved towards us and started firing at a distance of about 150 meters. Well-camouflaged Russian tanks were attacking the line of march. In the twinkling of an eye, everyone took cover in the ditches and watched the duel between our armored cars and the enemy tanks. A few antitank guns entered the fray and put an end to the uproar. After a few minutes we resumed the march. The burning tanks illuminated the night sky to our rear for a long time. At 1930 hours we exchanged the first rounds with the Soviets. In order to make sure we would accomplish the mission, I sent combat reconnaissance south, with orders to advance on Klevan via Olyka and wait for the battalion at Klevan.[5]

On 1 July the armies of the Southwestern Front received orders to pull back to the so-called "Stalin" Line, a fortified position built along the 1939 western border of the USSR. This was clear acknowledgement that the huge tank battle in the Western Ukraine had ended up in defeat for the Soviet side. Even though Kirponos managed to delay the German drive to Kiev for awhile, the losses sustained by his troops were shockingly heavy – by 8 July, for instance, the Front had fewer than 550 tanks.

Soviet infantrymen armed with Mosin–Nagant M1891 rifles and PPSh-41 submachine-guns in full readiness to defend Smolensk, beginning of July 1941. These soldiers, apparently, belonged to a reserve unit that was about to see its baptism of fire. (RIAN)

5 K. Meyer, "Grenadiers", Mechanicsburg, Stackpole Books, 2005.

A field repair of a damaged Pz III Ausf. F of Panzer-Regiment 4 (13. Panzer-Division) in the vicinity of Zhitomir, July 1941. (NAC)

T-26 Model 1933 tanks of the Soviet 105th Tank Division attack German positions, Western Front, July 1941. During the period in question the division was part of the army detachment of Major-General Rokossovsky. (Pressphoto)

Rokossovsky's corps was especially badly mauled – it was down to a mere 25 tanks and 11 armored cars. But the performance of its commander didn't remain unnoticed by the Stavka (the Soviet Supreme Command) – the 45-year-old General-Major was not only awarded the Order of the Red Banner, but on 15 July was appointed commander of an army detachment forming in the vicinity of Smolensk, where another crisis had developed.

SMOLENSK – MOSCOW – STALINGRAD

Smolensk's area was of critical importance to both belligerents, because it offered the shortest way to Moscow. Hitler attacked it with his most powerful formation, the bulk of Army Group "Center". Two task forces were formed, which advanced on a broad front to the northeast, along both banks of the River Dnieper. Their assignment was to encircle and destroy the Soviet armies deployed in the vicinity of the city, and subsequently to strike in the direction of the Soviet capital.

German troops stare at a burning building in Smolensk, July 1941. The soldier in the foreground is armed with a Karabiner 98k rifle. Two motor vehicles can be seen in the foreground: a Soviet GAZ truck and a German m.gl.Einheits-PKW (medium off-road passenger car). (NAC)

Stalin had entrusted the defense of the approaches to Moscow to one of his closest advisories, Marshal Semyon Timoshenko, appointing him commander of the Western Front. Timoshenko, himself a veteran cavalry officer, knew the qualities of Rokossovsky pretty well and, shortly upon the arrival of the latter, put him in charge of the Yartsevo sector (northeast of Smolensk), where the northern German pincer was trying to achieve a breakthrough.

Rokossovsky distinguished himself immediately. He not only managed to assemble his detachment from scratch (arriving reserves from the deep rear and leftovers of units previously decimated in Byelorussia), but also brought to a halt the advance of the enemy spearhead (7. Panzer-Division) and even recaptured Yartsevo in well-planned counterattack.

Determined to close the ring around the Soviet armies at Smolensk, *Generaloberst* Hermann Hoth, the commander of Panzer-Group 3, committed to battle two more panzer-divisions (12. and 20.) the men of Rokossovsky's detachment (which later would become known as the "Yartsevo" Group) withstood the pressure. They deserve credit for keeping open the so-called Yartsevo corridor for long enough to allow a

German troops armed with Karabiner 98k rifles engaged in heavy fighting in the vicinity of Smolensk, along the railway to Moscow, July 1941. A damaged Soviet KV-1 heavy tank loaded on a flatcar is about to become German booty. (NAC)

considerable number friendly troops to avoid entrapment. More importantly, Army Group "Center" was denied a rapid advance to the gates of Moscow. On the other hand, the bravery and self-sacrifice of Rokossovsky's troops didn't stop the Germans from sealing the pocket. The bulk of three Soviet armies were encircled and annihilated. About 300,000 Soviet troops ended up as POWs.

* * *

Following the slogging match at Yartsevo, the battle reached a stalemate and by the beginning of August both sides switched over to the defensive. The Germans and the Soviets spent the following two months in licking their wounds and preparing for the battles to come.

The tactical success achieved by Rokossovsky northeast of Smolensk earned him the reputation of "crisis-solver" and "fireman". He was appointed commander of the rebuilt 16th Army and promoted to Lieutenant-General.

On 5 October the Germans renewed their offensive on Moscow (Operation "Typhoon"). Shortly afterwards five armies found themselves trapped in a large pocket west of Vyazma and in the course of the next few days were annihilated. Rokossovsky's luck, however, remained with him and he avoided certain death or captivity. On 6 October he and his staff were ordered to hand over the divisions to the neighboring armies and immediately move to Vyazma to set up a new defensive position there.

Rokossovsky pictured shortly (or immediately) after his promotion to Lieutenant General, Vyazma area, September 1941. (RinP)

By mid-October the "new" 16th Army came under the command of the "new" Western Front now led by Marshal Georgy Zhukov, his former subordinate. It was those two extraordinary officers that would bring to a halt the so far invincible Nazi panzer armada and eventually would turn the course of the war.

The 16th Army was placed in the path of one of the main German striking forces, Panzer Group 4 of *Generaloberst* Erich Hoepner. Made once again from reserves that had just arrived from the rear and ad-hoc groups of units decimated in

An abandoned Soviet T-26 Model 1933 tank on Smirnov Square in the city center of Smolensk, July/August 1941. Road signs showing the location of the deployment areas of 10. Motorized Infantry Division (the capital F) and 18. Panzer-Division has been placed on its turret. Several trucks of Guderian's Panzer-Group 2 can be seen in the background. (Note the big capital G painted on each of them.) A heavy MAN Diesel vehicle is on the left of the photo. (NAC)

The spearhead of 2. Panzer-Division during the encirclement of the Soviet armies in the vicinity of Vyazma, the beginning of October 1941. The column consists of Pz III Ausf. J tanks and Sd.Kfz. 10 halftracks employed in a troop-carrier role. (NAC)

A column of Czech-built Pz 38(t) tanks of 7. Panzer-Division conduct a pincer movement that will lead to the encirclement of hundreds of thousands of Red Army troops in the Vyazma area, early October 1941. The tactical sign painted on the rear of the vehicle stands for Hoth, the commander of Panzer-Group 3. (NAC)

Pz III Ausf. J tanks of 11. Panzer-Division advance through a gap in the Red Army defense somewhere near Vyazma, the first half of October 1941. Soviet soldiers come forward to surrender with hands raised. (NAC)

the recent battles, the army was deployed along the Volokolamsk Highway with the mission of protecting the northwestern approaches to Moscow. Rokossovsky employed active defense tactics, retreating step-by-step towards the capital and counterattacking at every opportunity. Thus, between 12 and 15 November a combined task force made of infantry, tanks, cavalry and artillery delivered a series of powerful blows on the positions of 10. Panzer-Division at the village of Skirmanovo, some 8 km from the highway. Following some very fierce fighting, the Germans abandoned the place; both sides sustained serious losses.

On 16 November Army Group "Center" made one last-ditch effort to encircle and capture Moscow. The units of the 16th Army were not able to withstand the heavy enemy pressure delivered by five panzer-divisions (2., 5., 7., 10. and 11.) and were forced to fall back. Determined to save his troops from certain annihilation, Rokossovsky once again showed insubordination and disobeyed Zhukov's orders to stand fast. Instead, he intended to withdraw his divisions to more advantageous positions. When his proposal was rejected, Rokossovsky went over the head of the commander the Western Front and contacted directly Marshal Boris Shaposhnikov, the Chief of the Soviet General Staff. Having weighed up the situation, Shaposhnikov immediately sanctioned the retreat, which, in turn, infuriated Zhukov, who categorically forbade any retreat. As result of this, the 16th Army was pushed aside and the Soviet position northwest of Moscow was brought on the verge of collapse. But the Wehrmacht already had shot its bolt and before long Operation "Typhoon" stalled. In the first week of December 1941 the Western Front went over to the counteroffensive and the Germans began to retreat in disarray. By the beginning of January 1942 the 16th Army had recaptured all the ground as far as Volokolamsk. The fact that the 16th Army had taken the brunt of the Nazi effort to capture Moscow didn't pass unnoticed by Stalin – on 2 January 1942 its commander was awarded one of the highest Soviet decorations, the Order of Lenin, for exemplary military service.

The commander of the Soviet 16th Army, Lieutenant-General Rokossovsky (second to the left), member of the military council Lobachev and writer Stavsky examining abandoned German vehicles in the vicinity of Moscow, 10 December 1941. (RIAN)

"A picture worth a thousand words." This photo of a burnt-out Pz.Bef.Wg. III Ausf. E of 10. Panzer-Division and a dead German tanker clearly show the ferocity of the fighting on the approaches to Moscow in the fall of 1941. The machine was knocked out by the troops of Rokossovsky's 16th Army in the second week of November 1941, during the heavy battles for the possession of the area. (RIAN)

* * *

In mid-January 1942 the staff of the 16th Army was transferred to the left flank of the Western Front, where it took over some divisions from the neighboring formations. Thus, a completely new 16th Army came into being in the area northeast of Bryansk.

Rokossovsky's biggest success in that sector was the taking of Sukhinichi, a large junction on the Moscow – Kiev railway, which was bitterly defended by elements of the German 2. Panzer-Army. It was liberated on 29 January 1942 and shortly afterwards the frontline once again stalled west of the town. Rokossovsky himself was badly wounded on 8 March by a shell splinter and spent the next two and half months in military hospitals. (His ribs, lungs, liver and spine were either injured or bruised.) While recovering, he befriended Galina Talanova, a military doctor, who later became his mistress and with whom he had an illegitimate daughter in 1945.

The General returned to active duty on 23 May 1942. In June the 16th Army went over to the offensive once again, launching a powerful attack in the direction of Bryansk. For the first time the ground troops were supported by masses of combat aircraft, including dreadful Shturmoviks armed with unguided rockets. But the Germans had wisely used the quiet periods to improve their defensive positions and replenish their units, and succeeded in containing the Soviet onslaught. But the drawback didn't change the high opinion of the Stavka on one of the Red Army's proven "firemen" and on 13 July Rokossovsky was appointed commander of the Bryansk Front. This fact alone meant that now Rokossovsky belonged to the circle of Stalin's most trusted senior officers.

* * *

Rokossovsky's new assignment was to restore the situation in the vicinity of Voronezh, where the German Army Group "B" (*Feldmarshall* Fedor von Bock) had split the Southwestern and Bryansk Fronts and had captured most of the city by 8 July. Rokossovsky's predecessor Lieutenant-General Chibsov had failed to prevent the breakthrough of 4. Panzer-Army and was sacked only after a week. Rokossovsky, however, immediately proved that he was the right man for the job. On 16 July he launched a powerful counterblow with leftovers of the 5th Tank Army (less than 100 machines) into the German left flank in the area northwest of Voronezh. The counterattacks continued during the following days. Even though they were unsuccessful, they tied up for a while considerable enemy forces.

It is widely believed that the stubborn Soviet defense at Voronezh had to a considerable degree prevented the Germans from taking one of the most important objectives of their summer offensive, Stalingrad, already in August 1942. In particular, Hoth's 4. Panzer-Army went south seriously crippled, because two its most experienced formations (9. and 11. Panzer-Divisions) were pinned down by the resolute attacks of the left wing of the Bryansk Front and couldn't be relieved on time. They never rejoined Hoth's army. Furthermore, the inability of the German High Command to pull out 4. Panzer-Army in accordance to the time-tables gave Marshal Semyon Timoshenko, who was then in charge with the Stalingrad sector, at least two extra days, which he wisely used to strengthen his positions before the arrival of Hoth's tanks.

* * *

On 30 September Rokossovsky, most likely on Zhukov's urging, was appointed commander of the Don Front. The latter was made of six "pocket" armies and the 16th Air Army, and was deployed to the northwest of Stalingrad. It was opposed by some of the strongest formations of the German 6. Army, including 3. and 60. (Motorized) Infantry Divisions, and 16. Panzer-Division.

Throughout October the troops of the Don Front were involved predominantly in heavy local battles with several of the divisions of Generaloberst Paulus. The Soviet local attacks were usually unsuccessful, but at the same time they prevented the Germans from reinforcing their troops engaged in bloody street fighting in Stalingrad. On 19 October the bulk of Rokossovsky's armies launched a powerful offensive aimed at cutting off the rear communications of Paulus' 6. Army, but failed to break through.

By the end of October the Don Front was reduced to just three armies (24th, 65th and 66th), because it had been ordered to hand over two armies to its right-hand neighbor, the Southwestern Front. Nevertheless, Rokossovsky's formation was included in the Stavka grandiose plan to encircle and subsequently annihilated the Axis forces engaged in the Stalingrad area, Operation "Uranus". The Front was also replenished with men, ammunition and materiel.

"Uranus" kicked off on 19 November 1942. Two of Rokossovsky's armies took part in the onslaught: the 65th and the 24th. (Quite amazingly, the 65th Army of General Batov would remain a constant feature of all Fronts led by Rokossovsky till the VE Day.) Both armies played a secondary role in the grand offensive, but nevertheless managed to roll back to some extent the extreme left flank of 6. Army. One also has to keep in mind that unlike the Southwestern Front, which "shock"

Soviet senior officers (two lieutenant-generals and a major-general) inspect a captured German Pz III Ausf. L tank, Stalingrad area, late 1942. The machine initially had been used by 24. Panzer-Division (see the leaping horseman insignia clearly visible on the first photo), but later on, upon its repair in one of the field workshops, it was handed over to 14. Panzer-Division. There it was given a new turret number ('223') and the divisional insignia was painted right above it. Note additional (2 cm) frontal armored plate. (Andrei Gavrikov)

group encountered predominantly poorly armed and led Rumanian divisions, the 65th and 24th Armies had to deal with tough German troops.

The encirclement of 6. Army was completed on 23 November 1942. Between 250,000 and 300,000 Axis soldiers (Germans, Rumanians, Russian Hiwi) were trapped within an area measuring 50 km by 40 km. Their final annihilation was planned to begin shortly afterwards, but was postponed due to the German relief attempts (Operation "Winter Storm").

By 23 December it became clear that the German spearheads wouldn't be able to open a corridor to the encircled Axis group and able to hold out for long. Manstein, who was in charge of "Winter Storm" ordered the commanders of the panzer forces to end their attacks. Four days later Colonel-General Vasilevsky, the new Soviet Chief of General Staff, presented to the Stavka the plan for the final destruction of the surrounded 6. Army (Operation "Ring"). In the meantime the Don Front had beefed up (by absorbing the disbanded Stalingrad Front) and by the turn of the year already totaled seven field armies, plus the 16th Air Army.

Rokossovsky launched the "Ring" on 10 January 1943. Despite being short literally of everything, the starving German troops offered vigorous resistance and inflicted bloody losses on the attackers. (During the first three days of the offensive the Soviet armies lost about 25,000 men in killed and wounded, and many of its tanks.) They, however, were not able to hold out for long and the pocket gradually began to shrink.

The destruction of 6. Army was not completed yet when Rokossovsky received yet another recognition of his accomplishments – on 15 January he was promoted to Colonel-General. Moreover, two weeks later he was awarded the Order of Suvorov, 1st Class.

By the end of the month the sorry remnants of the once-invincible twenty two German divisions retreated back into the ruined city. On 2 February 1943 the German resistance in Stalingrad ceased for good. Paulus, who had just been promoted by Hitler to the rank of Feldmarshall, was taken prisoner along with about 91,000 of his troops. From that moment on Rokossovsky's military career skyrocketed.

Rokossovsky and Voronov (the supreme commander of the Red Army Artillery) interrogate Feldmarschall von Paulus, ca. 31 January 1943. (RinP)

CHAPTER 2

THE DEBACLE AT SEVSK

NEW ASSIGNMENT

On 4 February 1943 Rokossovsky was summoned to Moscow to receive his new assignment. He was driven from the airport directly to the Kremlin, where Stalin briefed him on the task. It was by no means an easy one – to thrust deep into the enemy rear and cut off the retreat routes of the German forces bitterly defending the so-called "Rzhev salient" (Model's 9. Army), capturing Orsha and Smolensk in the process.

Award ceremony in the Kremlin, early February 1943. The picture shows some of the heroes of the Stalingrad battle, who have just become recipients of the Order of Suvorov, 1st Class: (from left) Colonel-General Rokossovsky, Marshal of the Artillery Voronov, Lieutenant-General Tolbukhin (the commander of the 57th Army) and Lieutenant-General Gromadin (the commander of PVO, the Soviet anti-aircraft defense). Note that Tolbukhin still wears an old-style uniform without shoulder straps. (RinP)

The overambitious offensive, which would go down in history as the "Sevsk-Orel Offensive Operation" was set to begin on 15 February 1943. A newly-constituted force, the Central Front, which was raised from the nucleus of the Don Front, was to lead the way. It was made up of two of Rokossovsky's "Stalingrad" armies (21st and 65th), Don Front's tactical air force (the 16th Air Army) and two fresh formations – the 70th Army and the 2nd Tank Army – that had been raised anew. There were also a cavalry corps, artillery and anti-aircraft divisions, "Katyusha" rocket-launcher regiments and six independent (close-support) tank regiments. The Central Front seemed powerful on paper, but in reality it was by no means adequate to the task assigned to it. Worse still for Rokossovsky, nearly all of his forces were yet to arrive from various areas and places of the USSR, some of them very distant.

THE OFFENSIVE (FINALLY) KICKS OFF

The offensive was postponed several times and when it was finally unleashed on 25 February only part of the forces were deployed. Among them were 65th and 70th Armies, while the 2nd Tank Army rolled forward with only 182 of its 408 tanks. The participating troops were critically short of almost everything, especially of transport, ammunition and fuel. The weather and the terrain didn't favor them either – there

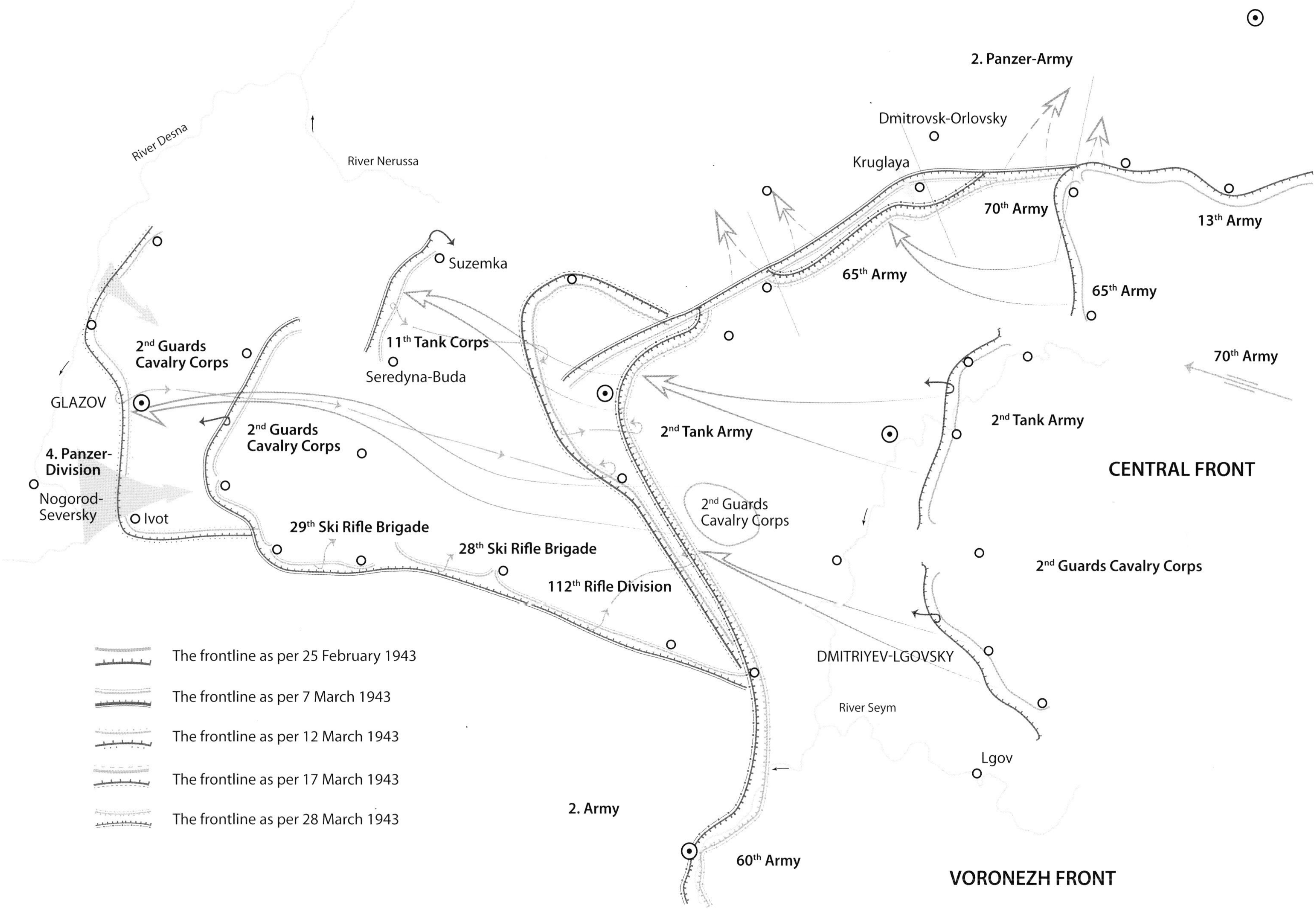

2. Panzer-Army
Dmitrovsk-Orlovsky
Kruglaya
70th Army
13th Army
65th Army
65th Army
River Desna
River Nerussa
Suzemka
11th Tank Corps
Seredyna-Buda
2nd Guards Cavalry Corps
GLAZOV
2nd Guards Cavalry Corps
4. Panzer-Division
Nogorod-Seversky
Ivot
70th Army
2nd Tank Army
2nd Tank Army
CENTRAL FRONT
2nd Guards Cavalry Corps
29th Ski Rifle Brigade
28th Ski Rifle Brigade
112th Rifle Division
2nd Guards Cavalry Corps
DMITRIYEV-LGOVSKY
River Seym
Lgov
2. Army
60th Army
VORONEZH FRONT
The frontline as per 25 February 1943
The frontline as per 7 March 1943
The frontline as per 12 March 1943
The frontline as per 17 March 1943
The frontline as per 28 March 1943

was only one motorway leading to the jump-off area and repeated snowstorms made off-road movement of vehicles impossible.

On Rokossovsky's right flank the 65th Army of Lieutenant-General Pave Batov made a relatively good progress against light resistance. This was made possible not only because its troops found a gap in the Axis frontline, but also because Batov's right wing was well protected by his neighbor to the northeast, the 13th Army of the Bryansk Front. The success of the army, however, was short-lived. The gradual withdrawal of the Germans from the Rzhev salient had created some reserves for operations elsewhere and *Feldmarschall* Günther von Kluge, the Commander-in-Chief of Army Group "Center", hurriedly moved them to Orel to restore his crumbling southern flank. Two of these reserve formations – 78. Assault-Division and 12. Panzer-Division – were placed in the path of Batov's army and by 28 February halted its advance at the outskirts of Dmitrovsk-Orlovsky.

Further south General Rodin's 2nd Tank Army fared no better. Considerably delayed by snowstorms and an insufficient road network, the army entered the battle piecemeal, literally one unit at a time. Its baptism of fire took place on 23 February, when most of the motorized infantry surged forward as simple foot soldiers, without any armored support (the tanks hadn't arrived yet) and very few artillery pieces. The Axis forces opposing them were a motley mix of low-grade German rear-security troops (707. Infantry Division), Hungarian anti-partisan forces (a regiment of 108. Light Infantry Division) and Russian collaborationist militias (the Kaminski Brigade). Having firmly entrenched themselves in the snow covered flatlands west of Kursk, they offered vigorous resistance right from the outset. It took Rodin's men four days of bloody fighting to overcome their resistance.

Meanwhile, one more combat-tested Soviet formation - 2nd Guards Cavalry Corps - had arrived. Very much like the rest of Rokossovsky's forces, it was considerably under-strength. For instance, one of the divisions had no horses at all and its soldiers would go forward through the snow as simple line infantry. Save for 8 mortars, the other of the divisions had no heavy weapons at all. There were no tanks either, since both tank regiments had been stranded by lack of fuel. The corps, nevertheless, got some reinforcements - three ski rifle brigades. Thus a pretty strange formation - the Kryukov cavalry-rifle group – came into being. It was made partially of mounted cavalrymen, some dismounted horsemen and ski-borne infantry, and had very few heavy weapons. But this was not the only problem that bothered Lieutenant-General Kryukov. The skiers, for instance, were absolutely exhausted and way beyond their physical endurance. They badly needed two days for rest and recuperation. But no commander could afford such a luxury.

The cavalry-rifle group entered the battle on the night of 24/25 February. It was committed to action immediately to the south of the tank army. The assignment of General Kryukov's cavalrymen was to ride straight to the west, towards Nogorod-Seversky, and secure the town. But it was by no means an easy one and the group advanced forward through the snow only with superhuman effort.

The tables turned in favor of the Soviets on 28 February, when at last some of the tanks of Rodin's army entered the battle. (Up to 50% of the tanks and artillery, as well one anti-aircraft division, an anti-tank artillery regiment and a regiment of "Katyusha" rocket launchers had to be left in the rear due to the total lack of ammunition and fuel.) On that day its 11th Tank Corps crushed the Axis resistance in the vicinity of Dmitriyev-Lgovsky and broke into open country. This had a domino effect on the German defense in that area and before long the entire southern wing of General Weiss' 2. Army collapsed.

On the afternoon of 1 March Rodin's assault detachments, in close cooperation with Kryukov's cavalry, captured the town of Sevsk, an important road junction, thereby cutting off the supply routes between 2. Army and 2. Panzer-Army. The Kaminsky's collaborationist brigade was nearly fully annihilated in the street fighting. During the next three days the offensive of the Soviet armored formation continued unabated. On 2 March they captured the town of Dmitriyev-Lgovsky and the Suzemka station, thereby cutting off the Konotop – Bryansk railroad. On the next day another key stronghold - Seredyna-Buda - was taken. The tank army also reported that it had inflicted serious losses on the Axis enemy: up to 6,000 troops were presumably destroyed, while some 1,500 others were taken prisoner.

The situation was developing in a direction that Rokossovsky hoped for. Stalin also saw in this an opportunity to regain the initiative in the center, where the Bryansk Front (Rokossovsky's right hand neighbor) had got stuck at the approaches of Orel. On the evening of 7 March he ordered the Central Front to turn its main forces (the 65th Army and the arriving 21st and 70th Armies) to the north and cut off the communications between Bryansk and Orel. By doing so, Stalin also intended to avoid another disaster, since Rokossovsky's penetration corridor was too narrow and therefore vulnerable to counterattacks.

In the meantime, the 70th Army of Major-General Tarasov, which had been recruited predominately of NKVD border guard troops, arrived after completing an exhausting 400-km-long march. It was under orders to attack to the north/northeast and sever the Orel – Bryansk railway, thereby helping its neighbors in encircling the German 2. Panzer-Army.

On 7 March the army got in touch with the Germans in the area to the east of Dmitrovsk-Orlovsky. The baptism of fire ended up in failure - *Feldmarschall* von Kluge had deployed there two battle-hardened formations (12. Panzer-Division and 258. Infantry Division) that met the inexperienced Soviets with hail of fire and resolute counterattacks. The fruitless offensive of the 70th Army continued till 18 March, but the German defense remained firm and gave no ground. But it was not only the lack of combat experience that prevented Tarasov's men from achieving a decisive breakthrough. It was revealed that they lacked physical stamina and were completely exhausted when they reached the battlefield. Worse still, as elsewhere, they were forced to attack with very little artillery support – the delivery of ammunition and the movement of the guns was considerably hindered by snowstorms, poor roads and lack of transport.

But the 70th Army was not the only one that experienced failure. Rokossovsky redirected the 2nd Tank Army, which assignment was to strike to the northeast and capture the town of Karachev. By doing so, he definitely hoped to restore the momentum, but only weakened his left flank and center, which soon would be struck by a sharp German counterthrust.

The fruitless offensive of Rodin's 2nd Tank Army north of Sevsk continued till 17 March. *Feldmarschall* von Kluge had quickly assembled there XXXXVII. Panzer Corps, which main forces (45. and 72. Infantry Divisions) were thrown into combat immediately after they detrained. The grenadiers, supported by all heavy weapons at their disposal, launched a series of resolute counterattacks and brought the Soviet armored units to a halt. On 19 March the tank army switched over to the defensive and on 24 March it was pulled out of the front to rest and recuperate.

On 11 March the Soviet Supreme Command disbanded the Bryansk Front and placed its former left flank (13th and 48th Armies) under the Central Front. Thus Rokossovsky's responsibilities were extended to include the sector south and southeast of Orel. But this didn't bring the dying offensive back to life. *Generaloberst* Rudolf Schmidt, the very experienced commander of 2. Panzer-Army, had consolidated his forces very well and all attempts of the Red assault teams to crush the Orel salient were beaten back with bloody losses. Further disappointment came from Moscow when Rokossovsky was informed that the detraining 21st Army would be shifted to the south, to Kharkov, where the Germans had launched a devastating counterblow. Thus, Rokossovsky was deprived of his main operational reserve, with which he would have been able to increase the weight of the attack.

The only formation that made relatively good progress during the second week of March 1943 was Kryukov's group, which still operated on Rokossovsky's extreme left flank. It moved through the gap between Weiss' 2. Army and Schmidt's 2. Panzer-Army, encountering only weak German and Hungarian units in its path. Heavy weapons on both sides were scarce and the fighting was limited predominantly to fire exchanges and hand-to-hand combat. By 10 March Kryukov's cavalrymen and ski-borne infantry reached the Desna River north of Novgorod-Seversky. This was the deepest Soviet penetration during the entire 1942/43 Red Army winter campaign.

THE GERMAN COUNTERATTACK

The rapid Soviet advance in the direction of Gomel raised serious worries in the German camp. Most of the rear zone of Army Group "Center" was now in danger. This called for urgent measures and they were taken immediately. Strong reinforcements (4. Panzer-Division and 251. Infantry Division) were hurriedly moved to Novgorod-Seversky to prevent the crumbling sector from falling apart.

It didn't take Rokossovsky and his staff long to figure out that the raid of the cavalry corps had shot its bolt. On 11 March the HQ of Central Front ordered Kryukov to go over to the defensive. But it was already too late to prevent the catastrophe that ensued. Let alone that Rokossovsky's order didn't help the cavalry-rifle group, but rather assisted the enemy counteroffensive. In particular, Kryukov was instructed to hold the entire area between Novgorod-Seversky and Sevsk by placing garrisons in all recently liberated towns and villages. Thus, the corps and the brigades were sliced into several detachments with little prospects of any effective coordination of their actions. (In other words, the Guardsmen and the ski infantry were thinly spread over a great distance.) Their situation was further complicated by the fact that they had very few heavy weapons and even less ammunition.

The Germans took full advantage of the situation. They simply bypassed the strongholds and then eliminated their garrisons by powerful concentric blows. *Leutnant* Lecius, a liaison officer in the HQ of 4. Panzer-Division, gives a clear explanation how this was done:

> It was a frosty, clear winter's day when the division commander climbed aboard his "goat" in order to personally lead the attack on [the village] Iwot for expanding the bridgehead of Nowgorod Ssewersk. Just before 0700 hours, he was in the

firing positions of "his artillery"; a short while later at the command post of Panzergrenadier-Regiment 12 next to a haystack 1 kilometer northwest of Iwot. At that time, the artillery preparation started on the village. All of the batteries, the attached Nebelwerfer, the antitank guns and the mortars fired and placed a fatal hail of fire on the enemy-occupied village. Within a short time, thick clouds of smoke rose to the heavens; the place was burning from one end to the other. Iwot was consumed by flames.

The plan to surround the village from all sides had succeeded, hopefully. The commander wanted to convince himself that all of the gaps had been closed. He moved along the eastern edge of the village in his "goat." Two Russians were retrieved from a stack of hay and disarmed. Based on the sound of the fighting, the enemy appeared to be well and heavily armed. You could hear the sound of the Russian submachine guns repeatedly. We received mortar fire. The General observed the village through the scissors scope as the Russians attempted to break out to the east. The tanks of the I./Panzer-Regiment 35 cut off their escape route. The ring around Iwot [Ivot] was solid.

The General moved back to the haystack. From there, he conducted a short telephone call with his operations officer and then moved into the village, where it was said that the command post of Panzergrenadier-Regiment 12 was located. The sounds of heavy fighting were coming from Iwot [Ivot]. No one seemed to know where Oberst von der Damerau was located at the time. The General thereupon took off into the village, moving between the glowing houses. The heat and the smoke took your breath away; the wind fired up the flames continuously. There were explosive sounds to the left and to the right. The grenadiers were clearing the village. Red Army men and partisans had barricaded themselves in practically every house and fired from ambush positions. *Leutnant* Broch fell victim to the bullet of a 15-year-old civilian.

The tanks continued to advance. They had to blast every building to bits before the resistance was broken. The command post for the 12th [Regiment] could not be located there. That meant we had to go back through the burning village until the Oberst was finally found in a side street.

The General wanted to take stock of the situation. He called *Oberst* Betzel and *Oberst* von der Damerau for a conference to that end at 0930 hours. The 1st Battalion was directed to immediately advance on Antonowka and take the village in the event of weak enemy resistance. Von Heyden's battalion was entrusted with the defense of Iwot [Ivot].

When the General went to the command post of Wüstner's battalion at 1030 hours, the

sound of the fighting had grown considerably weaker. The command post of the II./Panzergrenadier-Regiment 33 was located in a barn with a good view towards Kalijewka.

During a conference with Oberst Dr. Maus at Prukopowka, the General approved the recommendation of the regimental commander to move out on Kalijewka with Panzergrenadier-Regiment 33 in the afternoon.

Antonowka and Kalijewka were taken that same day.[6]

The main Axis counterattack began on 12 March. (Apart from the above-mentioned German forces, the Hungarian 105. and 108. Light Divisions also took part in it.) Overcoming the stiff enemy resistance, the grenadiers and the panzer troops pushed the Soviets all the way back to Sevsk. The fighting everywhere was brutal and some of the Red squadrons were wiped out to a man. By 20 March some of the remnants of Kryukov's group assembled in the vicinity of the town, while the rest remained in the Axis rear where they were completely surrounded. Most of them were subsequently annihilated.

Having no other choice left, General Krykov ordered his men to set up an all-around defense at Sevsk. In the meantime, the German pressure increased. The 3rd Guards Cavalry Division was hit especially hard. It was struck by about two regiments of infantry and up to 70 AFVs (including up to 30 tanks) that rolled forward on a very narrow front. The defenders already had lost more than 50% of their men and equipment, let alone that were critically short of artillery and anti-tank weapons. It was obvious that they wouldn't be able to hold out for long. On 27 March Sevsk was taken by the Germans; during the following two days they mopped up the last pockets of Soviet resistance in the town. Only some sorry remnants of the decimated cavalry regiments (groups of 20-30 men) managed to fight their way out.

* * *

One of the main reasons for the failure of the Sevsk-Orel Offensive Operation was that the Central Front launched its attack without any ideas how the troops would

6 H. Schäufler, "Knight's Cross Panzers", Mechanicsburg, Stackpole Books, 2010.

be supplied and repositioned. This is clearly confirmed by the recollection of Aleksei Voloshin, a battery commander with the 181st Rifle Division:

> With difficulty I made my way to Chelyabinsk, where the division was in the process of reforming. Soon we were loaded onto troop trains and at the end of February we disembarked in the vicinity of Elets. From there we conducted a ten-day rapid march to a point near Sevsk, where the Germans had encircled a cavalry corps. The regimental battery that I was commanding was being towed by horses, but we had only two horses per gun instead of the requisite four. At times the crews had to help haul the guns through the snow. It was hard. Snowdrifts blocked the roads. The local population was mobilized to clear the roads. Once we met Colonel-General Rokossovsky. He was driving by and stopped. He shouted, 'Who's the commander?' I went running up to him and reported, 'Lieutenant Voloshin, commander of a regimental battery of the 271st Rifle Division.'
> 'What's this? Why are you moving so slowly?'
> 'We don't have horses, and there are snowdrifts.'
> He drove off. The next day an order arrived: 'Get horses from the state farms. Give them a receipt, stating that their horses will be returned.'
> I remember going up to one collective farm chairman. He told me, 'We only have three horses.'
> 'We're taking them.'
> He pointed at one: 'This one's lame.' I ordered a soldier to lead the horse around. It in fact was lame. I told the chairman, 'We'll take two horses. Here's your receipt.' He had tears in his eyes. What was that slip of paper worth to him? He had to plough the fields within a month. That's how we scraped together horse teams for the battery.
> We approached Sevsk. Along the road we began to encounter dead horses on the left and right of it, all upside down – they'd frozen. We began to take the saddles from them. Our boots were now badly worn and in lousy shape. So we removed the saddles in order to make boots from the leather. That's what we did.
> The regiment took up defensive positions to the right of Sevsk. While on the defense, once the battery had to make a combat probe to obtain intelligence. In general, both we and the Germans fought poorly there. We were louse-ridden. In the rifle companies, half the men came down with typhus. I had eighty men in my battery, and half of them became sick. The spring was a cold one. The soldiers packed the available houses to the point where they were almost sleeping in several layers. At the end of March 1943, I also became sick.[7]

The negative outcome of the Sevsk-Orel Operation didn't shatter Stalin's trust in the Central Front's commander and on 28 April 1943 Rokossovsky was once again promoted in rank, this time to Army-General.

7 A. Drabkin (Ed.), "Panzer Killers", Barnsley, Pen & Sword, 2013.

CHAPTER 3

THE KURSK BATTLE

WAITING FOR THE STORM

The fall of Sevsk was the last nail in the coffin of Rokossovsky's ambitious operation. The fierce counterattack of 4. Panzer-Division, which was carried out in conjunction with the much more powerful counteroffensive of *Feldmarschall* von Manstein against the Soviet forces in the Kharkov-Belgorod area, put to an end the Red Army winter campaign. The belligerents were already pretty exhausted. Moreover, spring was arriving, bringing with it warmer weather and thaw, and both Stalin and Hitler realized that the time had come to switch over to the defensive. The legacy of the grandiose winter battle was a large Soviet bulge in the middle of the Eastern Front that would go down in history as the Kursk Salient. Not surprisingly, it immediately caught the attention of the German and Soviet Supreme Commands and became the natural focus of their strategic plans for the summer of 1943.

* * *

The Germans intended to eliminate the Soviet penetration already in mid-March 1943, when Rokossovsky's offensive was still in progress. The change of the weather, which brought the muddy season, as well as the lack of reserves, prevented that.

On 15 April Hitler issued Operational Directive No 6, which called for the Kursk offensive, codenamed Operation "Citadel", to begin on 3 May. The Führer and his aides were well aware that it was very important to attack before the enemy had a chance to prepare a defense in depth, with multiple mine barriers, trench lines and artillery emplacements. Operation "Citadel" was planned as a typical *Kesselschlacht* (cauldron battle). Two German task forces were to attack simultaneously in the direction of Kursk and seal off the salient, trapping inside the huge Soviet forces defending it (about five armies). The first task force was to be provided by von Manstein's Army Group "South" and was to consist of 4. Panzer-Army and Army Detachment "Kempf". The second force was to be provided by Army Group "Center" and was to be made of a single, but very powerful formation – 9. Army of *Generaloberst* Walter Model. The German 2. Army, still under the command of *Generaloberst* Walter Weiss, was to contain the western portion of the "bulge".

It is difficult to say whether Model was the best choice to lead such a large-scale offensive. After all, he had distinguished himself predominantly as a master of defensive warfare (he held the Soviets at bay at Rzhev for more than year), while his experience in offensive operations was limited to that of a leader of a panzer division. But in mid-April 1943 the other obvious candidate – *Generaloberst* Rudolf Schmidt, the commander of 2. Panzer-Army – was relieved of his post after the Gestapo arrested his brother, Hans-Thilo Schmidt, for spying for the French. (It is debatable whether an offensive led by Schmidt would have achieved better results.)

In terms of numbers 9. Army was super-strong. Model was to lead a force of sixteen infantry divisions, six panzer-divisions and a panzer-grenadier division, plus a number of close-support combat units. They were divided between five corps commands. Perhaps never before in the history of the German war machine had such a powerful force been gathered under a single army HQ. There was a problem, though – neither Hitler and his staff, nor Model were confident that "Citadel" would succeeded.

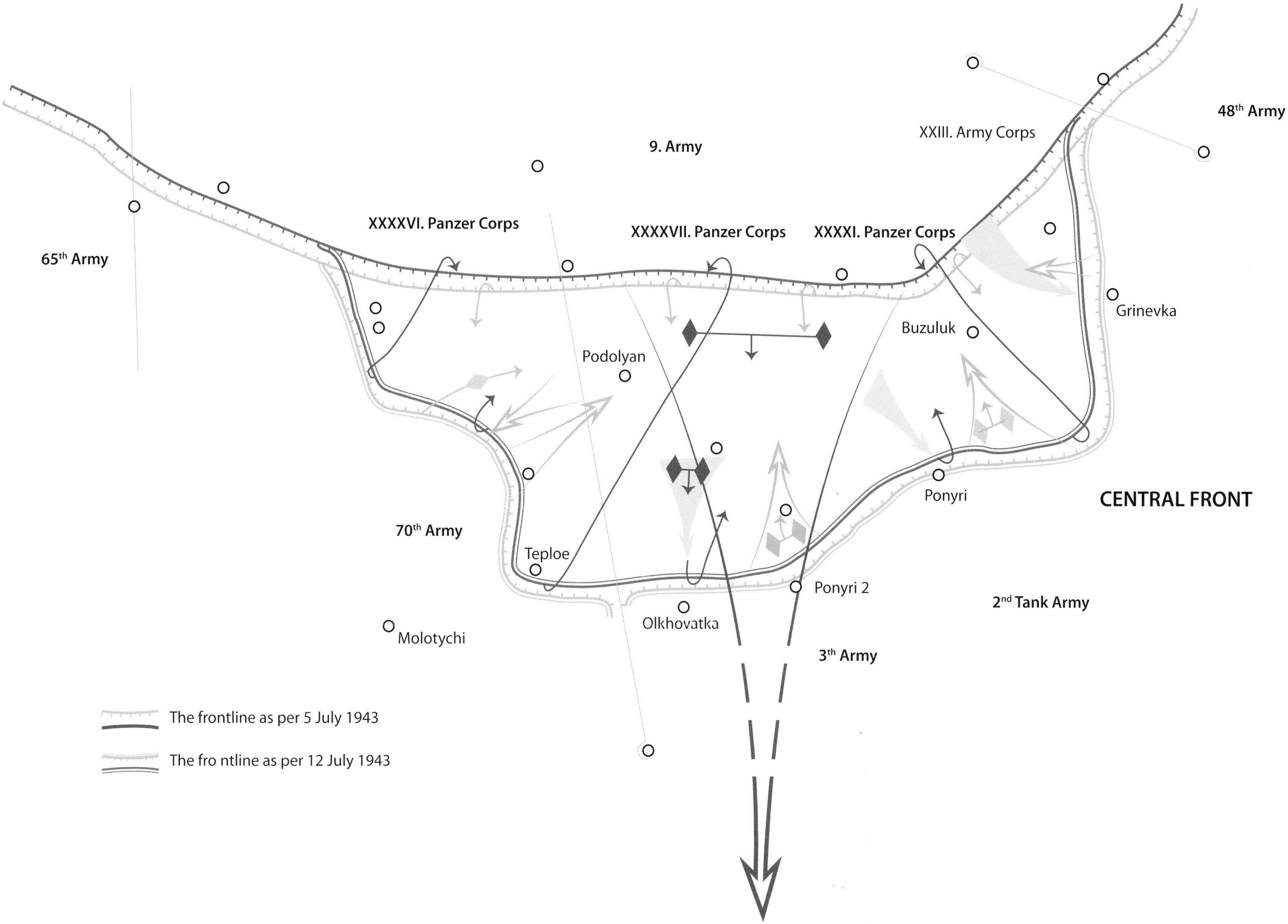
48th Army
XXIII. Army Corps
9. Army
65th Army
XXXXVI. Panzer Corps
XXXXVII. Panzer Corps
XXXXI. Panzer Corps
Grinevka
Buzuluk
Podolyan
70th Army
Teploe
Ponyri
CENTRAL FRONT
Ponyri 2
2nd Tank Army
Olkhovatka
Molotychi
3th Army
The frontline as per 5 July 1943
The fro ntline as per 12 July 1943

A Soviet anti-tank position on the northern face of the Kursk salient under intense German fire. The crew at the forefront operates 14.5-mm PTRD-41 anti-tank rifle, while the one in the background - 14.5-mm PTRS-41; the loader of the former is armed with Mosin–Nagant M1938 bolt-action rifle. An artillery piece, probably a 45-mm M1942 anti-tank gun, is clearly visible in the distance. (RIAN)

Their chief concern was the condition of the main assault forces. The panzer divisions, in particular, were still equipped with a large number of obsolete, under-gunned tanks like the Pz IIIs, let alone that they were considerably under-strength. In order to increase their combat value, they had to be urgently provided with as many Pz IV tanks mounting the more effective and longer 7.5 cm KwK 40 L/48 gun as possible. But the panzer divisions were not made only of tanks. Guderian, who had just been appointed General Inspector of Panzer Troops, had created a new concept for the basic organization of the panzer-divisions, which called for a large number of armored vehicles of all types. These included various types of halftracks, self-propelled howitzers and infantry guns, artillery observation tanks, recovery machines, flamethrower tanks, tank-destroyers and so on. Apart from that, special battalions equipped with Tiger heavy tanks, assault panzers and remote-controlled demolition vehicles were to be established. Needless to say, the urgent demand of so many tracked and half-tracked AFVs placed a heavy burden on German industry. On the top of that, most of these machines were new models and the crews operating them had yet to master them.

On 27 April, Model met with Hitler to discuss the details of the forthcoming operation. The General used the opportunity to express his concern about the enormous buildup found by the intelligence department. It was apparent that the Central Front was constructing very solid positions in the path of the planned offensive. Aerial reconnaissance also revealed that the main Soviet armored formations had been withdrawn into reserve. Model also expressed his worries that "Citadel" was becoming pointless since the longer the preparation for the operation continued, the lesser were its chances for success. He even dared to propose a complete cessation of all preparations for attack to focus on defeating of the Red Army summer offensive that inevitably was going to happen.

The next conference of the German senior officers involved in the planning of "Citadel" took place on 4 May 1943 in Munich. The offensive was nowhere near to begin and Hitler gave a long speech to justify its postponement. Then a number of possibilities were discussed, the main of them being:

- Going over to the offensive immediately with only the forces at hand
- Delaying the offensive even further to await the arrival of more tanks, and especially the newest models
- Cancelling the offensive altogether. The limited personnel and materiel resources of the Third Reich should be conserved and used to contain the forthcoming Soviet onslaught, as well as against the pending Allied invasion of Western Europe.

Strangely enough, one of those who favored an immediate attack was *Feldmarschall* von Kluge, the commander-in-chief of Army Group "Center" and Model's immediate superior. By doing so, he de facto dismissed the intelligence material of the 9. Army from a week before.

Among those who strongly supported the postponement of "Citadel" were Guderian and Albert Speer, the Minister of Armaments and War Production. Guderian, in particular, feared that the offensive would wear down his ambitiously reconstituted armored formations. Speer, in turn, did his best to explain the difficulties of rebuilding the panzer units and how the expected severe materiel losses would place a heavy burden on the industry.

Having weighed up the opinions of the participants, Hitler decided to postpone the offensive, but not to cancel it for good. He had his misgivings, but, nevertheless, decided to stay committed to the offensive. The Führer was realistically aware that "Citadel" was perhaps his last chance to turn the fortunes of the war on the Eastern Front. That's why he remained increasingly focused on the operation. But it was Hitler's dedication to the new weapons that he believed were the key to success of the assault – namely the Panther tank, the Ferdinand tank destroyer, as well as the greater numbers of the already proven Tiger tank – that went well beyond the point of obsession. That's why the repeatedly arriving intelligence reports about the increasing Soviet buildup in the Kursk salient forced him twice to move back the launch date of the attack, first to 12 June and later to the first week of July. Now Hitler was sure that the only way to breach the formidable Red defense was to allow as many AFVs as possible to reach the frontline formations.

A Pz III Ausf. N tank, presumably of 9. Panzer-Division, captured intact by the scouts of the Central Front. (RinP)

AFV STRENGTH OF THE PANZER-DIVISIONS OF 9. ARMY,
Beginning of July 1943

2. Panzer-Division: 12 Pz II, 40 Pz III, 60 Pz IV, 8 PzBef
4. Panzer-Division: 15 Pz III, 80 Pz IV, 6 PzBef
9. Panzer-Division: 1 Pz II, 38 Pz III, 38 Pz IV, 6 PzBef
12. Panzer-Division: 6 Pz II, 36 Pz III, 37 Pz IV, 4 PzBef
18. Panzer-Division: 5 Pz II, 30 Pz III, 34 Pz IV, 3 PzBef
20. Panzer-Division: 9 Pz 38 (t), 17 Pz III, 49 Pz IV, 7 PzBef

* * *

The intelligence of the Central Front was familiar with most of the divisions of Model's 9. Army. After all, until recently nearly all of them had belonged to 2. Panzer-Army and remained in place when Model took over the command of the sector in April 1943. What Rokossovsky didn't know yet was how strong they had become during the quiet period.

A column of T-34/76 (Model 1942) tanks with infantry mounted on them move into position, Central Front, July 1943. (TsAMO)

The perpetual delays in the German preparations allowed the Central Front not only to strengthen its defensive system, but to make it literally impregnable. Rokossovsky and his men didn't expect the lull in the fighting to last so long, but took full advantage of this unexpected luxury. They built a dense web of field fortifications, the sophistication of which would shock their opponents. Moreover, the positions were arrayed in depth and by the beginning of July three solid defensive belts came into being in the flat area north of Kursk.

The *Maskirovka* deception methods were also widely employed and nearly every fold in the ground was used to conceal and protect the troops. But it was the anti-tank defense that saw the biggest improvement. A tightly-packed network of carefully camouflaged anti-tank nests was established, with each nest consisting of several artillery pieces of various calibers. The nests were amalgamated with the minefields planted along the most likely avenues of German advance. (By the beginning of "Citadel" the average number of Soviet mines per kilometer of front reached the 3,200 mark.) Furthermore, the "avenues" in question were covered by the interlocking fire of the closest anti-tank guns. This would allow the defenders to draw the panzers into the so-called "fire pockets" exposing their most vulnerable parts.

A real hail of deadly fire awaited Model's troops right from the outset. Thus, each of the rifle companies occupying the main line of resistance was additionally reinforced with up to nine anti-tank guns, three artillery pieces, one tank (or self-propelled gun) and a platoon of combat engineers. More importantly, traditional weak points of Soviet combat performance, such as combined-arms tactics, cooperation between the different military branches, field communications, forward air control and precise fire direction were considerably improved thanks to the extensive training, command-staff exercises and drills.

A Soviet 57-mm ZiS-2 in action during the defensive battles north of Kursk, the first half of July 1943. Capable of penetrating 90-mm armor at a range of 1,000 meters, it quickly became one the deadliest enemies of German panzers. Due to its limited production (less than 10,000 pieces till the war's end), the gun was issued almost exclusively to the GHQ anti-tank artillery regiments and brigades. The ZiS-2 received its baptism of fire during Operation "Citadel". It is interesting to note that the Voronezh Front, which defended the southern face of the salient, didn't have any, while Rokossovsky's Central Front had four anti-tank regiments outfitted with them. From 5 to 12 July they fired more than 11,000 rounds on the approaching Germans. (TsAMO)

* * *

By the beginning of July 1943 the Central Front consisted of five field armies (60th, 65th, 70th, 13th and 48th), 2nd Tank Army and 16th Air Army, plus a number of independent units and formations. They numbered a total of 667,500 men, 1,745 tanks and self-propelled guns, 14,163 guns and mortars, and 1,092 aircraft. This meant that on the eve of "Citadel" Rokossovsky not only enjoyed a clear (at least two-fold) superiority over the opponent, but also that in the course of the battle he would be able to create strong operational/tactical reserves, with which to plug gaps and deliver counterblows.

THE GERMAN ONSLAUGHT

On 4 July 1943 the Germans launched a series of local, but powerful attacks against the southern face of the Kursk salient. The Soviets could virtually smell it in the air that something was brewing up.

Along the entire defensive perimeter of the Central Front it was still quiet, but reports about the German preparations kept coming in. In order to disrupt the enemy forces assembling for the attack, Marshal Zhukov (the Stavka coordinator) and Rokossovsky decided to launch a preemptive artillery bombardment. The powerful barrage was carried out shortly after midnight of 4/5 July, but results were less than hoped for.

Soviet infantrymen of 4th Guards Airborne Division in captured German foxholes during the Battle of Kursk, Central Front, July 1943. The crew in the forefront operates a Degtyaryov DP-27 light machine gun; the loader is armed with a PPSh-41 submachine-gun with a PPS-42 box-type magazine. The two soldiers occupying the other foxhole apparently are armed with Mosin–Nagant M1938 rifles. (TsAMO)

The offensive of Model's 9. Army began early in the morning of 5 July. It was preceded by a devastating 80-minute-long artillery preparation. Then the German assault detachments surged forward, aided by Stuka dive bombers. The 16th Air Army intervened immediately and right from the outset its pilots became involved in a series of dogfights with the Luftwaffe.

* * *

The main blow of 9. Army was delivered by XXXXVII. Panzer Corps of *General der Panzertruppe* Lemelsen. It rolled forward with 20. Panzer-Division (the only panzer-division of Model's army committed to battle on the first day of "Citadel") and 6. Infantry-Division, attacking toward Olkhovatka. While breaking through the Soviet main defensive positions, the grenadiers of the latter division were actively supported by the Tigers of Heavy-Panzer-Battalion 505 (45 tanks, some of them still in transit), as well as by a company of remote-controlled B IV demolition vehicles.

On the right flank, Lemelsen was supported by XXXXVI. Panzer Corps of *General der Infanterie* Hans Zorn (four infantry divisions and about 30 assault guns). They were to launch a secondary attack in the direction of Malakhova.

Lemelsen's left flank was covered by XXXXI. Panzer Corps of *General der Panzertruppe* Josef Harpe. Its two infantry division could count on strong armored support: Tank-Destroyer Regiment 656 (89 Ferdinand tank-destroyers, also known as "Porsche Tigers", and 45 Brummbär assault tanks) and the tank battalion of 18. Panzer-Division (about 80 tanks of various types). This massive task force was aimed at the town of Ponyri, a key Soviet stronghold near the Orel – Kursk railway.

To the left of XXXXI. Panzer Corps was XXIII. Army Corps, which main strength was concentrated in the 78. Assault (Infantry) Division (reinforced with more than 60 assault guns). The main exploitation force of 9. Army (five panzer-divisions and a panzer-grenadier division) was kept in reserve.

As one can see, Model intended to breach the three Soviet defensive belts in a classic "German" manner – in a very narrow sector, predominantly with infantry

Two knocked-out Ferdinand tank-destroyers of Tank-Destroyer Regiment 656 abandoned by their crews in the vicinity of Ponyri. The steel towrope attached to the vehicle in the forefront suggests that an unsuccessful attempt had been made to recover it. (TsAMO)

Two immobilized Ferdinand tank-destroyers of the Staff Company of Tank-Destroyer Battalion 654 (Tank-Destroyer Regiment 656) in the vicinity of Ponyri. The vehicle in the left (tactical number № II-03) was hit by a shell in the chassis and then set afire by Molotov cocktails. (TsAMO)

forces, assisted by break-through tanks and assault guns, plus heavy artillery and Luftwaffe close air support. By doing so he intended to "conserve" the strength of his panzer divisions as long as possible and unleash them only when the defense of the Central Front was fully breached. Then they would be moved through the breach and advance at full speed towards Kursk.

* * *

In the main breakthrough sector Lemelsen's two leading divisions (20. Panzer and 6. Infantry) struck hard the positions of the 13th Army north of Olkhovatka. From the very beginning their way forward was delayed by dense minefields. It took the German sappers more than two hours to clear passages in them. Then a weak point in the Soviet defense was found and the commander of 6. Infantry Division immediately redirected the Tiger battalion there. The penetrating assault of the heavy tanks and the grenadiers, which reached as far as the village of Butyrki, shattered the Soviet 15th Rifle Division and caused a serious crisis on the boundary between the 13th and 70th Armies. The situation of the former army was worsened by the failed armored counterattack at Butyrki, where 42 of up to 90 advancing T-34s were reportedly put out of action by the Tigers. The Germans, in turn, lost only two Pz VIs as total write-offs, with several others temporarily immobilized due to track damage.

The same machines as on the previous photo pictured from a different angle. (RIAN)

A Pz III Ausf. N tank hit by an armored piercing round is burning somewhere north of Kursk, July 1943. The machine presumably belonged to 9. Panzer-Division. (TsAMO)

A destroyed Pz IV Ausf. G tank of 8. Company/Panzer-Regiment 3 (2. Panzer-Division) somewhere in the Teploe – Olkhovatka area, July 1943. (TsAMO)

By late afternoon the spearheads of XXXXVII. Panzer Corps reached the second Soviet defensive belt where their advance de facto stalled. The fierce resistance put up by the forward units of the 13th Army had delayed the German divisions long enough to allow Rokossovsky to move forward some tactical reserves and plug the gap in the frontline. On top of that, the attacks of Lemelsen's assault detachments were once again halted by solid minefields. This time, however, the German sappers encountered greater difficulties when they tried to clear passages through them, because the approaches were covered by deadly artillery fire. The attempts to use B IV remote-controlled vehicles for mine-clearing were only partially successful. By nightfall the panzers and the grenadiers had gained nearly 10 km of ground, but Rokossvsky's main line of resistance remained intact.

Leutnant Hans Schäufler, platoon leader with Panzer-Signal Battalion 79 (4. Panzer-Division), shares with us his impressions of the first day of "Citadel" in the point of the main German effort:

> Unternehmen Zitadelle was intended to be the decisive battle on the Eastern front for 1943. It had been carefully planned for a long time, although it had been postponed several times. The dice would be tossed at Kursk. Based on the concentrated strength that we had, no one doubted that they would fall in our favor!
> The fireworks started on 5 July. It was intended for the infantry divisions, working together with the assault gun battalions, the Ferdinand regiment, which included Sturmpanzer-Abteilung 216, schwere Panzer-Abteilung 505, and the remote-control companies (that is, the Goliath companies), to clear a path through the deeply echeloned Russian defensive system for the tanks, which would follow.

A Tiger tank of Heavy-Panzer-Battalion 505 knocked out by the gunners of the Soviet 70th Army in the vicinity of Teploe. (TsAMO)

A crippled Ferdinand of Tank-Destroyer Battalion 653 (Tank-Destroyer Regiment 656) put out of action on 5 July 1943 by the 642nd Cannon-Artillery Regiment (5th Artillery Division) at Hill 257, not far from Ponyri. (TsAMO)

A Ferdinand of Tank-Destroyer Battalion 654 (Tank-Destroyer Regiment 656) knocked out by the Soviet artillery near Teploe. (TsAMO)

The interior of the same Ferdinand. (TsAMO)

> But the operation stood under an unlucky star from the very beginning. The Russians had been bombing our assembly areas for some time. According to the German Armed Forces Daily Report, 162 Russian aircraft were shot down on the first day alone. It is not too difficult to estimate the numbers of Russian bombers employed to unnerve our forces.
> The engineer forces of all of the divisions were consolidated in order to create lanes through the mines, since the Goliaths were unable to spread fear into the hearts of the Russians. [8]

Further to the east the spearheads of Harpe's XXXXI. Panzer Corps also succeeded in punching a hole in the first Soviet fighting position and by the evening reached the deserted town of Ponyri. (The civilian population of the area had been evacuated already by the end of April.) The limited success came at a cost: a large number of the Ferdinand tank-destroyers, which fulfilled the role of close-support AFVs, were immobilized by mines or enemy fire; the infantry battalions also sustained bloody losses. Thanks to the super-human efforts of the maintenance units, most of the Ferdinands were later recovered and repaired. No one, however, could bring the fallen grenadiers and engineers back from the dead.

Rokossvsky's resolve to defend Ponyri at all costs was easy to understand: the settlement was not only one of the cornerstones of the second defensive belt, but also was a major communication point that controlled virtually all roads and railways leading south to Kursk. Not surprisingly, during the following seven days it would become a scene of very fierce fighting.

The two corps forming the shoulders of Model's penetration corridor achieved far less. On the left flank of 9. Army the 78. Assault Division (XXIII. Army Corps) made a small inroad between the town of Maloarchangelsk and the Orel – Kursk railway. It would remain pinned down there by murderous enemy fire till the cancelation of "Citadel". On the western flank the XXXXVI. Panzer Corps tried to attack along the boundary between the Soviet 13th and 70th Armies. Its "shock" groups gained very little ground against the very determined Soviet resistance. The situation in that sector would remain unchanged during the next week or so.

A Pz III Ausf. M tank of 2. Panzer-Division put out of action from a distance of 550 meters by the 3rd Battery/872nd Howitzer-Artillery Regiment. Note additional frontal armored plate. (TsAMO)

8 H. Schaufler, "Panzer Warfare on the Eastern Front", Mechanicsburg, Stackpole Books, 2012.

* * *

Determined to prevent any further penetration of 9. Army, on the evening of 5 July Rokossovsky ordered an all-out counteroffensive to be launched on the next day. Nearly all available reserve forces would take part in it: the 2nd Tank Army, 19th Tank Corps and two Guards rifle corps. The 16th Air Army would provide the much-needed close-air support.

In the meantime Model, who was unaware of the scale of the Soviet preparations for counterattack, kept moving his reserves through the corridor. The 2. and 9. Panzer-Divisions, which had followed closely behind the spearheads of XXXXVII. Panzer Corps, were about to enter the battle in the morning. Thus, a large-scale clash of armor was going to take place and neither Rokossovsky, nor Model were aware of it.

The Soviet counterattack commenced early in the morning of 6 July after the usual preliminary artillery barrage. However, because of poor traffic coordination, only one of the formations of 2nd Tank Army (the full-strength 16th Tank Corps of Major-General Grigoriev) took part in it. It ran into the determined resistance of 20. Panzer-Division north of Olkhovatka and was literally shot to pieces, losing about half of its tanks. (88 machines were put out of action, most of them for good.) The surviving vehicles pulled back.

Later that morning, XXXXVII. Panzer Corps launched its own attack on Olkhovatka. It was spearheaded by the Tigers of Heavy-Panzer-Battalion 505, which Lemelsen had assigned to 2. Panzer-Division. The troops of the 17th Guards Rifle Corps, who had firmly entrenched themselves in this sector of the Soviet second defensive belt, fought back with great vigor. The advancing Germans were pinned down by the murderous fire and were not able break into the village.

Schäufler claims that the battle was a pure nightmare:

> On 6 July, the 2. Panzer-Division and schwere Panzer-Abteilung 505 moved out to attack. They broke through the first, second and third defensive lines, but they did not succeed in achieving the intended breakthrough to Kaschara. The Russians had apparently expected our attack at that point and at that time. After all, they had worked for months in excruciating detail to transform each meter, twenty-five kilometers in depth. Position after position had been built; antitank position after anti-tank position; tank after tank had been dug in on commanding

A Pz.Bef.Wg. III Ausf. H of 2. Panzer-Division knocked out by 12th Artillery Division in the vicinity of Lavrovka. (TsAMO)

The wreck of a German Pz III lost on 6 July 1943 at Buzuluk after it had been hit twice in the turret by 122-mm rounds fired by the 3rd Battery/642nd Howitzer-Artillery Regiment (5th Artillery Division). (TsAMO)

The image shows the three German panzers on the previous photos pictured together. (TsAMO)

A Pz IV Ausf. G of 2. Panzer-Division destroyed by several direct hits of 122-mm rounds fired by the 4th Battery/872nd Howitzer-Artillery Regiment from a distance of 600 meters. The southern limits of Soglasny, July 1943. (TsAMO)

> high ground by the hundreds. It was also there that he had established his ready reserves, large tank formations. On a sector fifteen kilometers wide, a tank battle ensued for which there had never been an equal. It was hard and merciless. [9]

In the afternoon Rokossovsky made one more attempt to push the Germans back. The 19th Tank Corps attacked in the direction of Podolyan, trying to cut off the "neck" of Model's penetration corridor. (This attack, actually, was to commence in the morning, simultaneously with the thrust of the 16th Tank Corps from the south, but it took nearly a full day to establish a close cooperation with the friendly infantry and to clear passages for the tanks in the minefields.)

The action turned out to be a total failure. The corps "bumped" into the same 20. Panzer-Division and also sustained serious losses: about 40 tanks of various types (Matildas, Valentines, T-70s and T-34s) were put out of action due to the murderous fire of the German artillery, panzers and strafing aircraft. Having witnessed the fruitless attempts of his men to overcome the dogged enemy resistance, Major-General Vasiliev (the corps' commander) had no other choice but to order a retreat.

The fighting at Ponyri, the sector where Harpe's XXXXI. Panzer Corps was attacking, was no less intense. Harpe's two infantry divisions and 78. Assault Division were now joined by 9. Panzer-Division, but even this didn't help the Germans in breaking into the heavily fortified town. The Soviet formation holding the place, the 307th Rifle Division, fought doggedly for every meter of ground. The infantrymen were not alone in their desperate struggle against the panzers, Ferdinands and assault guns. They received massive support from the artillerymen and the T-34s of the 3rd Tank Corps.

Vasily Grossman, a prominent Soviet writer and war correspondent, visited Ponyri on that day. Having already seen a lot of combat, he nevertheless, was shocked by the ferocity of the fighting. Grossman later wrote in his notes:

> Visit to Ponyri. Shevernozhuk's regiment. Stories about 45-mm cannons firing at [Tiger] tanks. Shells hit them, but bounced off like peas. There have been cases when artillerists went insane after seeing this. [10]

* * *

Even though at first glance it seemed that the counterattacks of the Central Front were useless, they actually bought Rokossovsky time to redeploy his forces along the second defensive belt, bring forward reserves, strengthen the weak points and pull out two of the shattered divisions from the frontline. This proved to be the turning

9 Schäufler, "Panzer Warfare on the Eastern Front".

10 V. Grossman, "A Writer at War", London, The Harvill Press, 2005.

A captured T-34/76 (Model 1943) used by the Germans during Operation "Citadel". It was destroyed on 5 July 1943 in the vicinity of Alexandrovka by the 4th Battery/753rd Cannon-Artillery Regiment (12th Artillery Division).

A Pz IV Ausf. G of 2. Panzer-Division knocked out by the 76-mm guns of the 7th Battery/124th Light Artillery Regiment at Mayskaya Zorka, 7 July 1943 (12th Artillery Division). One of the rounds had destroyed the left track. (TsAMO)

A Pz IV Ausf. G shot to pieces at the northern limits of Shirokoe Boloto on 6 July 1943. It was hit in the right side of the chassis by 122-mm rounds fired by 5th Battery/239th Howitzer-Artillery Regiment (5th Artillery Division). (TsAMO)

A Pz III Ausf. N tank of 2. Panzer-Division knocked out by 76-mm armor-piercing rounds fired by the ZiS-3 guns of 7th Battery/1007th Light Artillery Regiment (5th Artillery Division) near Mayskaya Zorka, 6 July 1943. (TsAMO)

A Pz IV Ausf. G of 4. Panzer-Division knocked out in the Samodurovka – Teploe area. (TsAMO)

point of the battle on the northern face of the Kursk salient. During the following six days the German 9. Army wouldn't be able to gain any significant ground and eventually "Citadel" would be canceled.

By nightfall of 6 July, however, the German senior commanders still believed that victory was possible. Model asked *Feldmarschall* von Kluge for additional reinforcements (12. Panzer-Division and 10. Panzer-Grenadier-Division) with which to exploit the success of the first-wave assault formations. His new plan called for the setting up of two "shock" groups: one under Lemelsen's XXXXVII. Panzer Corps (2. and 4. Panzer-Divisions) and one under Harpe's XXXXI. Panzer Corps (86. and 292. Infantry-Divisions). The former was to strike to the southwest, towards Teploe, while the latter was to push to the southeast, towards Ponyri. But the plan had a drawback: instead of creating a *Schwerpunkt* (a point of main effort), Model would keep attacking in divergent directions and by doing so would further disperse his formations.

* * *

On 7 July the fighting along the second Soviet defensive belt continued unabated. Model committed to action the main body of 18. Panzer-Division, thereby increasing the pressure in the vicinity of Ponyri. Supported by heavy weapons, the grenadiers succeeded in capturing half of the town after brutal house-to-house fighting. But Rokossovsky already had deployed there a mortar brigade and an anti-tank artillery regiment, and the intended decisive breakthrough failed to materialize. The 307th Rifle Division managed to contain all further German attacks and the rest of the fortified place remained in Soviet hands.

On 8 July both Rokossovsky and Model threw into the battle their last operational reserves, the 9th Tank Corps and 4. Panzer-Division, respectively. The fresh forces allowed the Soviet 13th Army to launch a sharp counterattack already in the morning and recapture Ponyri.

This particular Soviet success proved to be only temporary, however. Over the course of the next three days both sides wrestled for possession of Ponyri, undertaking a series of powerful local attacks and counterattacks. The slogging match continued till 10 July and by then the Germans had retaken most of the town. The nearby Hill 253.3 witnessed equally heavy fighting, but the stalemate remained unbroken.

The Germans, in turn, were not that successful in their efforts to breach the second Soviet defensive belt. Even the commitment of the rested 4. Panzer-Division didn't help them in overcoming the resolute enemy resistance.

Leutnant Reinhard Peters, platoon leader with I./Panzer-Regiment 35, vividly recalls the entry of the division into the battle:

> After weeks of a break for resting, which our 1st Battalion spent in Karatschew, it was time. During the first few days of July, we moved into the area around Liwny. The major summer offensive was about to start. During the night of 7/8 July, we moved to our attack positions. We had never seen such a concentration of armored forces before. Fortunately, Ivan had not noticed us, since it would have been a tempting target for Soviet bombers.
> 8 July, 0230 hours — We received the order to move out. The objective was Hill 240 at Teploje. Wing after wing of the Luftwaffe thundered overhead—bombers, Stukas, bombers, Stukas. And so it went for hours on end. All of them dropped their payloads on the hill. The Stukas also attacked individual targets, the dug-in T-34's and KV I's on the forward slope of the hill. That calmed our nerves, since nothing could go bad after that.
> Georgi's company initially took point. When our tanks exited the defiles at Ssamodurowka, they received bitter antitank-gun and main-gun fires. We had not expected that after the gigantic bombing raids. The first attack wave started to waver. After the next tank company also bogged down in the defensive fires, it was our turn. *Oberleutnant* Prast issued the order to attack, but he was knocked out after advancing only a couple of hundred meters. *Leutnant* Beck, the senior platoon leader, assumed acting command of the company, but his command was also of short duration. After a few minutes, his tank was also hit. Then it was my turn. I ordered: *"Panzer—marsch!"*
> But there weren't too many of us. Only a few vehicles were rolling next to me. Oberfeldwebel Allgaier had identified a dug-in KV I, one of many. With his Swabian steadfastness and calm, he took it in his sights. But the distance was too great; the 7.5-centimeter main-gun round ricocheted off. He then fired in front of the tank with high-explosive rounds, so that the kicked-up dust and dirt would rob the enemy of visibility. He used the time to get closer. The same game was repeated two or three times. Then he was where he wanted to be. He waited in ambush with an antitank round in the breech. The clouds of dust dissipated, and the target was revealed. On the way! Target! It was masterful.
> As a result of the hours of massed bombing and shelling, there was a cloud of gunpowder smoke and dust above us. The sky seemed to be masked off. I felt it was the afternoon, but my watch only showed 0900 hours. In the meantime, Petrelli's company had reached the village of Teploje, which lay at the foot of the hill. Our attack started to bog down again, however. For the first time, we experienced the employment of Goliaths, small, remotely controlled tracked vehicles with demolitions mounted on them. But they didn't quite work as planned. Due to technical problems, they would not operate or they were knocked out. In any case, they did not bring success.
> We breathed a sigh of relief, when we saw Sauvant's [505th] Tiger battalion pull up. We needed reinforcement and relief. Just as I was edging over the top of the commander's cupola to observe with my binoculars, a monstrous pressure, accompanied by an ear-deafening bang, threw me from my commander's seat. It was now our turn, I thought. But we were all in one piece, including the tank. The reasons were soon found. A Tiger had taken up position behind my Panzer IV. When it fired, the muzzle of the 8.8-centimeter main gun was barely a meter from my open commander's hatch. That wasn't exactly the way we had conceived the Tigers would be employed.
> The afternoon saw an immediate counterattack on the part of the Russians. We pulled back to the edge of a defile and waited. A Russian tank unit rolled about

A burnt-out Pz IV Ausf. G put out of action in the Samodurovka – Teploe area. (TsAMO)

A Sturmpanzer IV Brummbär assault tank of Assault-Panzer Battalion 216 (Tank-Destroyer Regiment 656) destroyed by a direct hit of 152-mm round in the Ponyri area, July 1943. (TsAMO)

A disabled Ferdinand of Tank-Destroyer Battalion 653 (Tank-Destroyer Regiment 656) put out of action on 9 July 1943 by the 8th Battery/100th Super-Heavy Howitzer-Artillery Regiment (5th Artillery Division) at Hill 257, near Ponyri. One of the 203-mm super-heavy rounds had blown off the left track. (TsAMO)

A Ferdinand of Tank-Destroyer Battalion 653 (Tank-Destroyer Regiment 656) knocked out by the Soviet artillery near Ponyri, July 1943. (TsAMO)

A Marder III Ausf. H open-topped tank-destroyer knocked out on 10 July 1943 near the Ponyri train station by the 9th Battery/753rd Cannon-Artillery Regiment (5th Artillery Division). (TsAMO)

A Ferdinand '502' of Tank-Destroyer Battalion 654 (Tank-Destroyer Regiment 656) disabled by a mine near the village of Goreloe, the Ponyri area. (TsAMO)

1,000 meters to the left of us. We were able to take it under effective flanking fires. The rest were eliminated by the Tigers. But Russian infantry also attacked at the same time. They approached us through the grain fields with stoic calm. It was swarming with them in front of us. We let them approach to within 300 meters, then it was "Fire at will" with our machine guns and high-explosive rounds. The attack was bloodily repulsed.

During the night, an element of Petrelli's company succeeded in making it to the top of the highly desired Hill 240. But the tanks had to pull back at first light. The key position of the enemy could not be taken. It was a black day for the battalion. In the log books of the battalion maintenance sergeant were many entries listed as total losses at Teploje on 8 July 1943.[11]

* * *

On 9 July a staff conference was held with Kluge, Model, Lemelsen and Harpe at the HQ of the XXXXVII Panzer Corps. After hearing the reports, it became clear to the German commanders that the 9. Army was lacking the effective strength to achieve the desired breakthrough, and, apparently, the enemy had realized this already. Having weighed all pros and cons, Kluge, nevertheless, decided to continue the pressure on the Soviets in order to support the offensive of the friendly forces (Manstein's Army Group "South") against the southern face of the Kursk salient.

On 10 July Model made one last attempt to penetrate the Soviet second defensive belt. XXXXVII Panzer Corps attacked the area between Teploe and Olkhovatka with the combined might of three of its panzer-divisions (2., 4. and 9.), plus the Tigers of Heavy-Panzer-Battalion 505. Up to 300 tanks, assault guns and armored halftracks struck the Soviet positions. As elsewhere, Rokossovsky's well-entrenched men met the advancing AFVs and infantry with murderous fire and their attack stalled.

Again Schäufler tells us what Model's last-ditch effort to crush the Soviet defense looked like:

Unternehmen Zitadelle. It meant death . . . it meant blood . . . it drove us to despair! We were running against a wall of fire and steel . . . against a forest of anti-tank guns . . . a gauntlet of artillery . . . a defensive bulwark of enemy tanks. Unternehmen Zitadelle. It gave us a sense of dread.

11 Schäufler, "Knight's Cross Panzers".

A Ferdinand '501' of Tank-Destroyer Battalion 654 (Tank-Destroyer Regiment 656) put out of action on 5 July 1943 by the 7th Battery/208th Howitzer-Artillery Regiment (5th Artillery Division) at Hill 243, the Ponyri area. The left track of the vehicle was blown off by a 122-mm round. (TsAMO)

The fighting between Soborowka and Ponyri raged back and forth. There were about 1,000 tanks fighting on each side. Generalfeldmarschall Model ordered an attack with all means available.

On 10 July, our 4. Panzer-Division rolled forward en masse. The division commander, General von Saucken, accompanied the attack in the first wave in his command-and-control vehicle, DO 1. He always led from the front and rallied his tankers and infantrymen to follow him. It was possible to penetrate into Teploje. During an advance, the general's vehicle collapsed the span of a bridge. It was unable to either back up or move forward. The signals officer, my friend *Leutnant* Simon, was badly wounded while looking for a way to recover the vehicle, and he remained lying out in front of the friendly lines. *Leutnant* Lecius, the division commander's aide, wanted to help him and was mortally wounded in the head in the process.

By field-expedient means — a fragile voice radio connection — the division commander led his division from that exposed position. On top of the other bad luck, the division operations officer, *Oberstleutnant* Lutz, was also badly

A Sturmpanzer IV Brummbär assault tank of Assault-Panzer Battalion 216 (Tank-Destroyer Regiment 656) blown apart by a direct hit at the Ponyri train station, 9 July 1943. The kill was credited to 9th Battery/753rd Cannon-Artillery Regiment (5th Artillery Division). (TsAMO)

The wreck of a Pz IV Ausf. G at Hill 248.5 near Ponyri. The tank was lost on 8 July 1943 when it was hit twice in the turret by 152-mm rounds fired by 1st Battery/86th Heavy Howitzer Artillery Brigade. (TsAMO)

This Ferdinand of Tank-Destroyer Regiment 656 had been hit by a heavy high-explosive aerial bomb released by a Pe-2 dive bomber, the Ponyri train station, July 1943. (TsAMO)

A Pz III Ausf. J and two Ferdinands abandoned by the Germans at Ponyri on 8 July 1943 after they fell victim to the combined direct-laying fire of the 6th Battery/642nd Corps-Cannon Artillery Regiment and 4th Battery/540th Light Artillery Regiment. (TsAMO)

A Pz III Ausf. L knocked out on 9 July 1943 at Hill 253.5 by the 76-mm ZiS-3 guns of 3rd Battery/697th Light Artillery Regiment (5th Artillery Division). (TsAMO)

German infantry weapons and equipment abandoned after a sudden Soviet artillery barrage somewhere north of Kursk, Central Front, July 1943. In the photo, one can see an 8 cm Granatwerfer mortar, and plenty of Model 1924 Stielhandgranate hand grenades and machinegun ammunition boxes. (TsAMO)

A StuG III Ausf. G assault gun put out of action by Soviet artillery in the vicinity of the Maloarchangelsk train station, Central Front, July 1943. Note the victory kill rings painted by the crew on the barrel. (TsAMO)

wounded at nearly the same time at the division command post. The commander of Panzer-Aufklärungs-Abteilung 4 was killed. [...]
From there, the terrain sloped gently down towards Teploje. We needed to go there with our lines. It was not too far, but it was as if we were on a silver platter. We were without cover and had to move directly to the feet of the Russians.
Out of the haze behind the houses, dark like a gigantic log, was the ridgeline where the Russians were positioned and could observe the flat-as-a-board terrain and dominate it with their weapons. They were firing at every individual man. There was absolutely no way to take the direct route. And if it were indeed possible to get through the line unscathed, then it would be clearly impossible to maintain it. It would be interrupted all the time—shot to pieces or chewed up by tank tracks—and no line troubleshooter would get through unscathed during the day.

A totally destroyed German Sd.Kfz. 8 prime mover of an unknown Luftwaffe unit (presumably Flak), Central Front, mid-July 1943. The kill was credited to 2nd Battery/496th Howitzer Artillery Regiment. Note the machinegun belts spread over the vehicle. (TsAMO)

> A Russian trench line ran along the ridgeline about a hundred meters behind us. It was filled with dead men. We crawled along on our backs with the field wire over the bloated corpses and forced our way through the collapsed trenches. Just don't raise your head above the edge of the trench, because it would start blazing from up above—and they didn't always miss their mark. [12]

The relentless German attacks at Ponyri also didn't bring the desired clean breakthrough. According to Guderian, one of the main reasons for that was the poor design of the monstrous Ferdinand tank-destroyers that were used in lieu of the traditional assault guns:

12 Schäufler, "Panzer Warfare on the Eastern Front".

A StuG III Ausf. G assault gun lies in pieces after receiving several direct hits from Soviet 152-mm large-caliber shells, Ponyri area, July 1943. (TsAMO)

> I visited both the attacking fronts during the time between the 10th and the 15th of July. I gained an insight into the course that events were taking, the lack of our men's experience in the attack, and the weaknesses of our equipment. My fears concerning the premature commitment of the Panthers were justified. Also the ninety Porsche Tigers, which were operating with Model's army, were incapable of close-range fighting since they lacked sufficient ammunition for their guns, and this defect was aggravated by the fact that they possessed no machinegun. Once they had broken into the enemy's infantry zone they literally had to go quail shooting with cannons. They did not manage to neutralize, let alone destroy, the enemy rifles and machine-guns, so that the infantry was unable to follow up behind them. By the time they reached the Russian artillery they were on their own. Despite showing extreme bravery and suffering unheard-of casualties, the infantry of Weidling's [86. Infantry] division did not manage to exploit the tanks' success. Model's attack bogged down after some 10 kilometers. [13]

13 H. Guderian, "Panzer Leader", London, Macdonald Futura Publishers, 1980, p. 311.

A Tiger I tank of Heavy-Panzer-Battalion 505 knocked out by the guns of the 1st Guards Artillery Division near the village of Molotychi, north of Kursk, July 1943. (TsAMO)

Two German Pz IV Ausf. G tanks of 2. Panzer-Division destroyed by one of the regiments of the 40th Anti-Tank Artillery Brigade during the "Citadel", July 1943. (TsAMO)

Pz IV Ausf. G tanks of 2. Panzer-Division shot to pieces by the guns of the 40th Anti-Tank Artillery Brigade, Central Front, July 1943. (TsAMO)

A Pz IV Ausf. G of 2. Panzer-Division knocked out by the 40th Anti-Tank Artillery Brigade, Central Front, July 1943. (TsAMO)

In a desperate attempt to change something, on the next day Kluge reinforced Model with two more mobile formations from his reserve: 12. Panzer-Division and 10. Panzer-Grenadier-Division. They were employed on the shoulders of the penetration corridor: the 12th Panzer attacked the Soviet positions at Tagino, while the 10th Panzer-Grenadier relieved the badly mauled 292. Infantry-Division at Ponyri. But these moves, however, proved too little and too late to reverse the fortunes of war.

On 12 July the Soviet Bryansk Front launched Operation "Kutuzov", the Red Army full-scale offensive on the Orel salient, which immediately endangered the left flank and the rear communications of 9. Army. The critical situation required an urgent redeployed of at least some of the armored formations employed by Model, since the last two panzer-divisions still kept by Kluge in reserve (5. and 8.) were by no means enough to check the Soviet onslaught. Within hours, Model's six panzer-divisions (2., 9., 12., 18. and 20.) disengaged and were rushed to the crumbling front northeast of Orel. Thus, "Kutuzov" sounded the death knell for "Citadel".

In his postwar memoir, Guderian clearly explains how the failure of the offensive ruined the defensive strategy of the Third Reich:

> By the failure of Citadel we had suffered a decisive defeat. The armored formations, reformed and re-equipped with so much effort, had lost heavily both in men and in equipment and would now be unemployable for a long time to come. It was problematical whether they could be rehabilitated in time to defend the Eastern Front; as for being able to use them in defense of the Western Front against the Allied landings that threatened for next spring, this was even more questionable. Needless to say the Russians exploited their victory to the full. There were to be no more periods of quiet on the Eastern Front. From now on the enemy was in undisputed possession of the initiative. [14]

14 Guderian, op.cit., p. 312.

General der Panzertruppe Joachim Lemelsen, the commander of XXXXVII. Panzer Corps. (NAC)

General der Infanterie Hans Zorn, the commander of XXXXVI. Panzer Corps. (NAC)

A Pz IV Ausf. G tank of 2. Panzer-Division shot to pieces by the guns of the 40th Anti-Tank Artillery Brigade, Central Front, July 1943. (TsAMO)

German heavy artillery pieces (10.5 cm leFH 18M howitzer and 8.8 cm Pak 41 anti-tank gun) captured by the 70th Army during the August-1943 counteroffensive of the Central Front. (TsAMO)

Soviet crew (members of 5th Battery/478th Mortar Regiment) load the barrel of their 120-mm mortar during the opening days of the Chernigov-Pripet Operation, late August 1943. The photo was taken in the vicinity of Sevsk, in the sector of the 65th Army. (Valery Zamulin)

CHAPTER 4

BOBRUISK

FROM KURSK TO BYELORUSSIA

The spectacular success of the Central Front at Kursk earned Rokossovsky yet another very prestigious military decoration, the Order of Kutuzov, 1st Class. The official award recommendation was signed on 27 August 1943, when the battle was long over. By then the armies of the Front already had cleared the southern part of the Orel salient and had just launched another strike in the general direction of Gomel.

The actual offensive kicked off on the day before the official announcement of Rokossovsky's award. The Central Front was still very strong on paper (it comprised five armies, a tank army, an air army and two independent armored corps), but in reality the heavy battles at Kursk and Orel had taken heavy toll on its main combat formations. Not surprisingly, the initial Soviet attacks quickly bogged down in the face of the determined resistance of the German 2. Army. But the staff of the Front once again displayed exemplary flexibility and immediately recognized where the problem was coming from. Wasting no time, Rokossovsky transferred the 13th Army (reinforced with the 9th Tank Corps) about 100 km to the south, to the Front's extreme left flank, where the enemy defense was much weaker.

The movement was executed in the best possible manner. Both the foot soldiers and the mechanized units used strict noise and light discipline during the difficult night marches and the German intelligence lost track of the two formations. This allowed Rokossovsky to deliver a powerful blow in the south while most of the German reserves (i.e. panzer divisions) were still in the north. The Soviet attack caught 2. Army completely off guard and *Generaloberst* Weiss had no other choice left, but to order a full-scale retreat.

By 5 September the armies of the Front already had advanced 125 km to the west, taking many prisoners and capturing plenty of materiel in the process. On 21 September Rokossovsky's left flank reached the Dnieper at Chernigov and by the end of the month the Central Front was already in possession of three large bridgeheads on the western bank of one of largest European rivers. The two strongest German army groups on the Eastern Front, "Center" and "South", were effectively separated and loose connection between their inner flanks was maintained with great difficulty.

In early October 1943 the two armies of Rokossovsky's left flank were placed under the neighboring Voronezh Front. At the same time his right flank was extended to the north by incorporating three armies of the disbanded Bryansk Front. By doing so the Stavka de facto shifted the main axis of advance of the Central Front from the southwest (Kiev) to the northwest (Minsk). Quite logically, on 20 October it was officially re-designated the Byelorussian Front.

* * *

The actions of the Front on Byelorussian soil didn't proceed as planned. The terrain was marshy, there were many forests and the road network was insufficient. Shortage of ammunition occurred once again, but it was the very skilful resistance of the Germans and the mobile defense tactics employed by them that played a key role in the defensive success of Weiss' 2. Army.

54

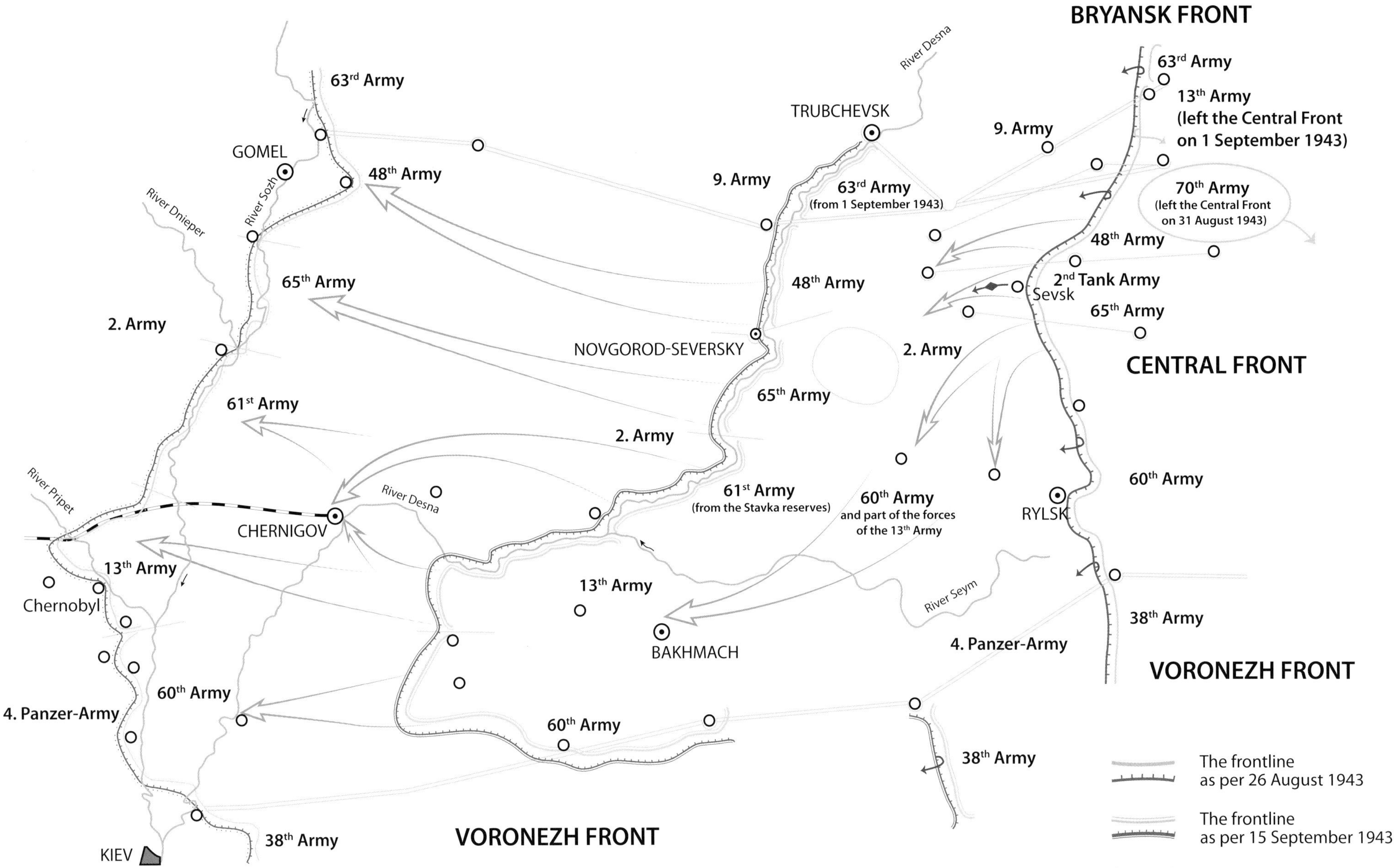
BRYANSK FRONT
63rd Army
13th Army
(left the Central Front
on 1 September 1943)
9. Army
70th Army
(left the Central Front
on 31 August 1943)
48th Army
2nd Tank Army
Sevsk
65th Army
CENTRAL FRONT
2. Army
TRUBCHEVSK
River Desna
9. Army
63rd Army
(from 1 September 1943)
48th Army
NOVGOROD-SEVERSKY
65th Army
2. Army
61st Army
(from the Stavka reserves)
60th Army
and part of the forces
of the 13th Army
RYLSK
60th Army
River Seym
38th Army
4. Panzer-Army
VORONEZH FRONT
13th Army
BAKHMACH
60th Army
38th Army
63rd Army
GOMEL
48th Army
River Sozh
River Dnieper
65th Army
2. Army
61st Army
River Pripet
CHERNIGOV
River Desna
13th Army
Chernobyl
60th Army
4. Panzer-Army
38th Army
KIEV
VORONEZH FRONT
The frontline
as per 26 August 1943
The frontline
as per 15 September 1943
The frontline
as per 1 October 1943

A German Pz IV Ausf. H tank destroyed by one of the units of the 4th Artillery Corps of the Byelorussian Front in the vicinity of Kalinkovichi, January-February 1944. (TsAMO)

A German supply truck destroyed by the artillery of the 1st Byelorussian Front during the Rogachev - Zhlobin Operation, late February 1944. (TsAMO)

From mid-October 1943 to the end of February 1944 Rokossovsky's armies launched up to seven powerful offensives in the northwesterly direction, but gained very little ground at the cost of heavy losses in men and materiel. Employing up to six panzer divisions (2., 4., 5., 12., 16. and 20.) the Germans repeatedly counterattacked along the boundary between their 2. and 9. Armies. The Soviets captured Gomel (26 November), Mozyr (14 January) and Rogachev (24 February), but failed to reach Bobruisk and therefore were not able to deliver the desired decisive blow in the direction of Minsk.

In April 1944 the Stavka disbanded the short-lived 2nd Byelorussian Front and incorporated its armies into the 1st Byelorussian Front. (The Byelorussian Front was officially re-designated 1st Byelorussian Front in late February 1944.) By doing so the Soviet Supreme Command extended Rokossovsky's zone of responsibility to include Kovel and the Pripet Marshes. At same time it provided Rokossovsky with more options, because now he was able to create not one, but two "shock" groups, one at Kovel and one at Bobruisk.

In view of the Stavka intentions to launch the main summer offensive in Byelorussia, the Front was massively reinforced. During May and June it received the 8th Guards Army (from Bessarabia), 28th Army and 4th Guards Cavalry Corps (from the Ukraine), 2nd Tank Army (from Rumania) and 1st Polish Army (from the Stavka reserves).

In late May 1944 Stalin summoned most of the commanders of the Fronts facing Army Group "Center" (only General Petrov, the commander of the "new" 2nd Byelorussian Front, was not present) to a planning conference in Moscow. The officers of the Operations Department of the General Staff presented their preliminary concept, which called for encircling and annihilating the bulk of the enemy forces in a large pocket east of Minsk. The main blows were to be delivered by the spearheads of the 1st and 3rd Byelorussian Fronts along converging motorways leading toward Minsk. Upon linking up at the Byelorussian capital, they were to chase the remnants of the Army Group "Center" as westerly as possible. In the meantime, the 2nd Byelorussian Front would attack straight from the east to mop up the pocket. The grandiose strategic offensive was codenamed "Bagration" after the famous Russian military leader in the war against Napoleon.

Apart from the main attack in the direction of the Byelorussian capital, Rokossovsky intended to conduct a local double envelopment at Bobruisk, using two field armies and two tank corps to surround the main body of the German 9. Army in the vicinity of the town. If Rokossovsky can be believed, the dictator bitterly opposed the plan at first, but eventually was persuaded to approve it.

For the time being the "shock" group on the Front's left flank at Kovel was to remain inactive. Subsequently, it was to launch a deep thrust in the General direction of the Vistula.

* * *

The Bobruisk "shock" group consisted of four armies (28th, 65th, 48th and 3rd), two tank corps (9th and 1st Guards), the cavalry-mechanized group of Lieutenant-General Pliev (4th Guards Cavalry Corps and 1st Mechanized Corps), the 16th Air Army and the Dnieper Flotilla. Both tank corps were fully equipped with the latest version of the famous T-34, namely the T-34/85, while the mechanized corps was outfitted with Lend-Lease M4 Sherman machines.

AFV STRENGTH OF THE SOVIET TANK CORPS BY THE BEGINNING OF THE BOBRUISK OPERATION,
June 1944

1st Guards Tank Corps: 210 T-34, 21 SU-76M, 21 SU-85
9th Tank Corps: 209 T-34, 21 SU-76M, 21 SU-85

The Kovel "shock" group, which was still in the process of deployment, was made of four Soviet armies (70th, 47th, 8th Guards and 69th), the 1st Polish Army, the 2nd Tank Army (three-tank-corps-strong), 11th Tank Corps and two cavalry corps (2nd Guards and 7th Guards). As with the other "shock" group, the four tank corps waiting in disguise at Kovel were fully equipped with T-34/85s.

The 61st Army, which was holding a very wide frontage in the Pripet Marshes, was also to remain passive during the opening stage of "Bagration"; it was to serve as a bridge between the "shock' groups.

* * *

The 1st Byelorussian Front faced approx. half of the Army Group "Center" (2. and 9. Armies). The critical Bobruisk area, which was under constant Soviet pressure since the autumn of 1943, was entrusted to 9. Army of *General der Infanterie* Hans

StuG III Ausf. G assault guns (different versions) knocked out by the 40th Anti-Tank Artillery Brigade of the 1st Byelorussian Front on the Rogachev – Madary road, 22 February 1944. (TsAMO)

Soldiers of the 1st Byelorussian Front have a short break after some very intense fighting, early April 1944. The sentry operates a Degtyaryov DP-27 light machinegun. The soldier in the right is armed with AVS-36 automatic rifle with 15-round magazine, while the other two – with PPSh-41 submachine-guns with drum magazines. Two of the soldiers also have RPG-40 anti-tank hand grenades attached to their belts. (RIAN)

Jordan. By mid-June 1944 it consisted of ten infantry divisions divided between three army corps, plus one security and one panzer (20.) divisions kept in reserve. The latter, actually, was the sole armored formation at the disposal of *Feldmarschall* Ernst Busch, the commander of the army group. Given that about five panzer-divisions had managed to contain Rokossovsky's previous offensives only at the cost of great efforts, it was not difficult to conclude that a single panzer-division stood no chances against the Red armored armada assembled in Southeastern Byelorussia. But why had such negligence occurred?

The OKH, and especially its intelligence branch, FHO (known as Foreign Armies East) fell victim of the grand Soviet deception measures. Till the last days of June the FHO kept predicting that the main Soviet summer offensive would take place in Northwestern Ukraine and nowhere else. That's why the best-equipped panzer-divisions were held in reserve at Kovel or to the south of it till the outbreak of "Bagration".

Speaking of 20. Panzer-Division, it must be noted that by the beginning of the Soviet offensive it was at full strength. On the other hand, it was somewhat crippled by the absence of two key elements (the tank-destroyer battalion and the armored reconnaissance battalion, as well as by the fact that it had only one panzer-battalion instead of two. (The division had about 80 serviceable tanks, predominantly Pz IVs.)

THE SOVIET BOBRUISK OPERATION

The offensive of the right wing of the 1st Byelorussian Front began at dawn on 24 June. The artillery delivered the usual powerful barrage. The 16th Air Army joined the battle only at midday, when the weather improved. It launched a series of devastating attacks on the German positions and ground communications, in which not only nearly all serviceable Il-2 Shturmoviks but also 224 level bombers took part. Save for some Flak guns and auto-cannons, the Germans had no arguments against such an overwhelming force.

The Bobruisk pocket, late June 1944. Wreckage of destroyed German equipment. One can see a StuG III Ausf. G assault gun (bottom left), a Steyr 1500 light truck (middle) and an RSO tractor (right). (TsAMO)

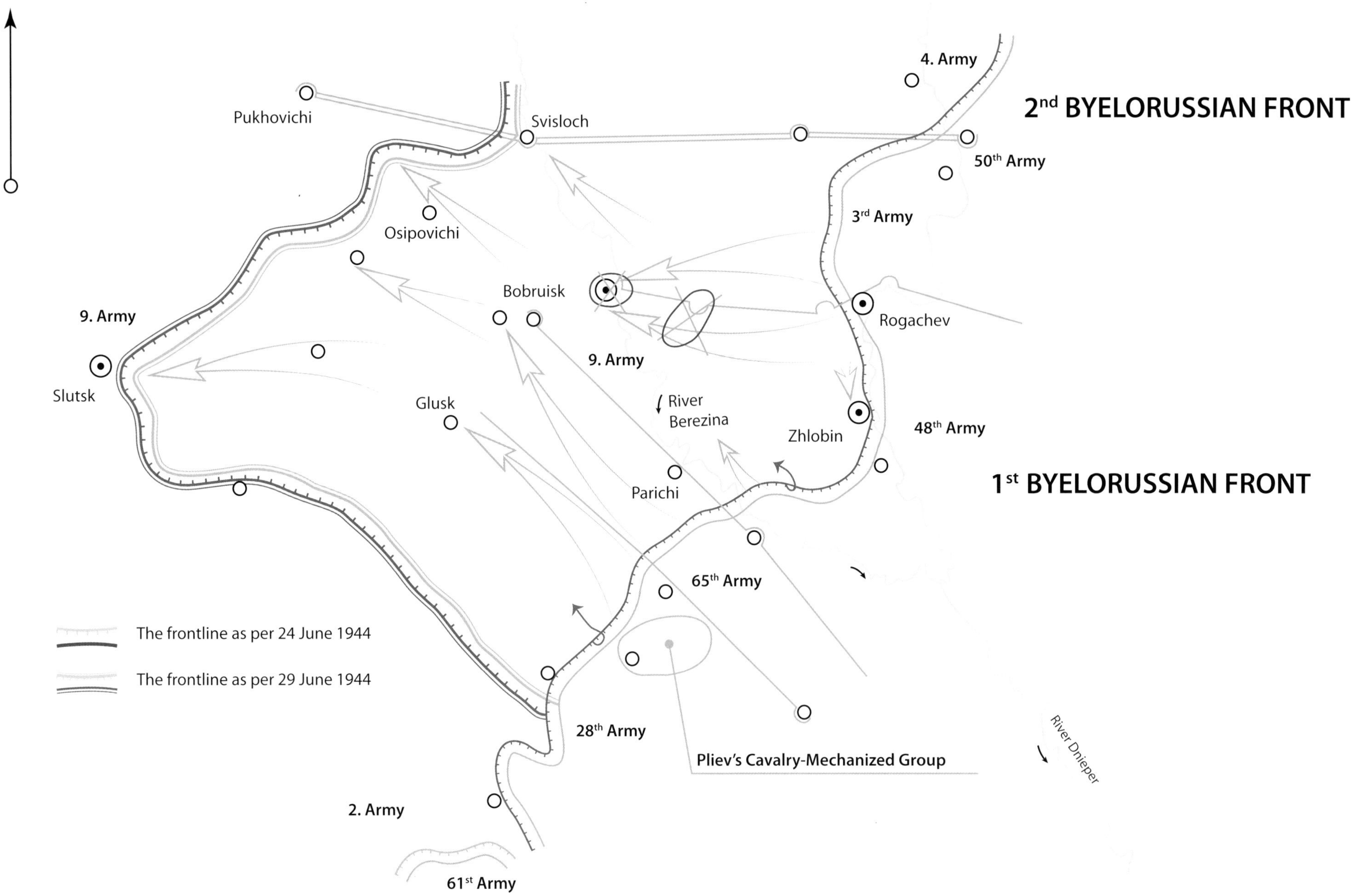
4. Army
2nd BYELORUSSIAN FRONT
Pukhovichi
Svisloch
50th Army
3rd Army
Osipovichi
Bobruisk
Rogachev
9. Army
Slutsk
9. Army
River Berezina
Glusk
Zhlobin
48th Army
1st BYELORUSSIAN FRONT
Parichi
65th Army
The frontline as per 24 June 1944
The frontline as per 29 June 1944
28th Army
Pliev's Cavalry-Mechanized Group
River Dnieper
2. Army
61st Army

The Bobruisk pocket, late June 1944. Wreckage of destroyed German equipment. A smashed 8.8 cm Pak 41 anti-tank gun at the forefront. (TsAMO)

The Bobruisk pocket, late June 1944. Wreckage of destroyed German equipment. A knocked out Horch 901 staff car is in the right. (TsAMO)

The Bobruisk pocket, late June 1944. Wreckage of destroyed German equipment. Two abandoned German anti-aircraft guns – an 8.8 cm Flak 36/37 heavy piece and a 3.7 cm Flak 37 auto-cannon - are clearly visible. (TsAMO)

The Bobruisk pocket, late June 1944. Wreckage of destroyed German equipment. One can see an Sd.Kfz. 251 Ausf. D (of 20. Panzer-Division) halftrack, a StuG III Ausf. G assault gun and a Steyr 1500 light truck (right). (TsAMO)

The Bobruisk pocket, late June 1944. Wreckage of destroyed German equipment. An abandoned Sd.Kfz. 2 Kettenkrad tractor is at the forefront. (TsAMO)

The Bobruisk pocket, late June 1944. Wreckage of destroyed German equipment. A burnt-out Marder III Ausf. M tank destroyer is at the forefront. One also can see a knocked-out Sd.Kfz. 10 soft-skinned halftrack (left) and a badly damaged Sd.Kfz. 7/1 self-propelled quadruple anti-aircraft auto-cannon (right). (TsAMO)

The forces operating to the west of the Berezina River – 28th and 65th Armies – made a deep penetration already on the first day of the offensive. They advanced up to 10 km to the northwest, liberating about 50 settlements in the process. The good progress of the first-wave units allowed General Batov, the commander of the 65th Army, to unleash his main exploitation force, the 1st Guards Tank Corps. The mission of the latter was to surge forward at full speed and cut off the retreat path of the Bobruisk garrison. This task was accomplished on Day 3, when the spearheads of Batov's army reached the riverbank of the Berezina south of the town. Their actions were actively supported by the gunboats of the Dnieper Flotilla. (The vessels, in particular, landed a party at Parichi, and by doing so succeeded in eliminating one of the main strongholds on the approaches to Bobruisk, the village of Zdudichi.) In the meantime, the 28th Army of Lieutenant-General Luchinsky crossed the Ptich River near the town with the same name.

* * *

The dangerous penetration of the Soviet 65th Army forced General Jordan to transfer there his sole mobile reserve, 20. Panzer-Division, which had just begun a successful counterattack in the sector of XXXV. Army Corps. The division was turned 180 ° and then drove more than 100 km over poor roads during the night of 24/25 June before it finally reached the area of XXXXI. Panzer Corps on the other side of the Berezina. When at dawn of 25 June the panzers and the grenadiers arrived at Parichi, the gap in the German frontline was already 40 km. Even though the troops of 20. Panzer-Division reported the destruction of nearly 60 Soviet tanks, it was already too late to prevent the collapse of the defense of XXXXI. Panzer Corps. *Generalleutnant* Edmund Hoffmeister, the corps' commander, had no other choice left, but to order his badly battered divisions to conduct a fighting withdrawal toward Bobruisk.

* * *

The offensive of the Soviet troops operating to the east of the Berezina progressed at a much slower rate. The initial attacks of the two Soviet armies (3rd and 48th) against the positions of the German XXXV. Army Corps achieved very little. Thus, on the morning of 24 June the assault detachments of the leading two rifle corps of the 3rd Army managed to break only into the first and the second trench lines. All their attempts to advance further were checked by resolute German counterattacks backed by AFVs. The 48th Army fared no better. The vast marshy wetlands along both sides of the Drut River delayed the crossing of the infantry and considerably hampered the maneuverability of the tanks. It took the assault detachments about two hours to clear the first trench line (often in hand-to-hand combat) and only by midday succeeded in securing the second one. Since the offensive in the sector of Gorbatov's 3rd Army had achieved greater results and therefore offered better prospects for a decisive breakthrough, Rokossovsky decided to shift the main effort to the north. The 9th Tank Corps was redirected there and entered the battle on the afternoon of 24 June.

The Soviet onslaught east of Bobruisk was considered very dangerous and in the afternoon General Jordan committed his only armored reserve, 20. Panzer-Division in the sector of XXXV. Army Corps. During the evening of 24 June the armored vanguard of the division counterattacked the spearheads of the 9th Tank Corps and achieved some success. But, as it was already mentioned above, the worsening situation to the south of Bobruisk forced General Jordan to order the panzer-division to disengage and hurriedly to transfer to the other side of the Berezina to clear out the penetration of the enemy 65th Army.

* * *

On 25 June Rokossovsky introduced to battle the Pliev Cavalry-Mechanized Group. It was unleashed in the sector of the 28th Army and, wasting no time, advanced to the northwest. On the next day the cavalrymen and the tankers reached the Ptich in the vicinity of Glusk and at several places even succeeded in crossing that river. Further to the east the 1st Guards Tank Corps also made a deep penetration into the German rear and by midnight of 26/27 June already had blocked all the roads leading from Bobruisk to the southwest and west. Both mobile formations received constant close support from the 16th Air Army, which units strafed and bombed the retreating German units, as well as the crossings over the Berezina, without mercy.

In the meantime, the troops of the extreme right flank of the 1st Byelorussian Front continued to experience problems. Despite the overwhelming superiority in men and materiel, they were still not able to overcome the very determined resistance of the German XXXXI. Panzer Corps. In a desperate attempt to turn the tables in his favor, on the morning of 25 June General Gorbatov, the commander of the 3rd Army, released his main exploitation force, the 9th Tank Corps. The brigades of Major-General

The Bobruisk pocket, late June 1944. Wreckage of destroyed German equipment. A burnt-out RSO tractor can be seen in the middle. (TsAMO)

The Bobruisk pocket, late June 1944. A bridge over the Berezina hastily built by German engineers lays destroyed after the Shturmoviks ruthlessly strafed the traffic on it. (TsAMO)

The Bobruisk pocket, late June 1944. Wreckage of destroyed German equipment. A knocked-out hybrid Pz III Ausf. L with an Ausf.H chassis of 20. Panzer-Division is in the right. Note also the fixed StuG III type fenders. (TsAMO)

The Bobruisk pocket, late June 1944. Wreckage of destroyed German equipment. Abandoned heavy weapons lay along the road: two heavy field howitzers without the barrels (in the background) and a 12 cm Granatwerfer 42 mortar (in the right). (TsAMO)

The Bobruisk pocket, late June 1944. Wreckage of destroyed German equipment. Soviet soldiers stare at decimated supply trucks, staff cars and horse-drawn carts. (TsAMO)

Bakharov displayed great skill and, despite the marshy, forested terrain, managed to break out into open country. As elsewhere, they were effectively supported by the Il-2 Shturomviks of the 16th Air Army. On the morning of 27 June Bakharov's spearheads began to outflank Bobruisk to the north and shortly afterwards established contact with the southern pincer, the 1st Guards Tank Corps of the 65th Army. Thus, a considerable part of the German 9. Army – eight divisions (or their elements) and a number of service and support units totaling up to 70,000 men - was encircled in the vicinity of the town. By then the main body of the 65th Army also had reached the gates of Bobruisk, while the 28th Army had secured Glusk.

The surrounded German troops made desperate attempts to break out and link up with their neighbor to the left, 4. Army of *General der Infanterie* Kurt von Tippelskirch (also trapped in the vast forested area between Orsha and Mogilev). Together, both armies had to establish a common front along the Berezina and contain the Soviet onslaught on the distant approaches to Minsk. But it was not meant to be.

The Bobruisk pocket, late June 1944. Wreckage of destroyed German equipment. A column of 20. Panzer-Division hit hard by the Soviet artillery and air force. Among the immobilized vehicles one can see a burnt-out Hummel self-propelled howitzer, an 8.8 cm Flak heavy anti-aircraft gun (in the left) and a Pz IV tank (in the middle). (TsAMO)

The Bobruisk pocket, late June 1944. Wreckage of destroyed German equipment. A staff omnibus hit by Soviet fire. (TsAMO)

The surrounded German divisions at Bobruisk found themselves pressed from all sides and squeezed into an ever diminishing perimeter. But it was the massive air strike delivered by more than 500 Red aircraft that broke their will. The devastating aerial raid lasted about 90 minutes, inflicting heavy losses on the defenders and spreading panic among them. Many German soldiers simply tossed away their weapons and tried to sneak through the Soviet blocking detachments in small groups or individually. But only very few succeeded.

By midday on 28 June the main body of the 48th Army broke into the outskirts of Bobruisk. The German garrison managed to contain the Soviets for a while, but within a day was completely decimated by concentric attacks from several directions. The still intact elements of the garrison launched a breakout under the cover of night, but only a small group, several thousand-strong, managed to escape in the direction of Osipovichi.

Vasily Grossman, the renowned Soviet war correspondent, visited Bobruisk immediately after the conclusion of the battle. As usual, he vividly describes the scenes he had encountered there:

The Bobruisk pocket, late June 1944. Wreckage of destroyed German equipment. Soft-skinned and armored vehicles immobilized by Soviet artillery and strafing aircraft. Knocked-out vehicles lay along the main road. (TsAMO)

The Bobruisk pocket, late June 1944. Wreckage of destroyed German equipment. Soft-skinned and armored vehicles immobilized by Soviet artillery and strafing aircraft. Among them one can see a self-propelled howitzer, probably a Hummel (top left), and StuG III Ausf. G assault gun (middle). (TsAMO)

The Bobruisk pocket, late June 1944. Wreckage of destroyed German equipment. Trucks of various models abandoned in a hurry by the retreating units of 9. Army. (TsAMO)

The Bobruisk pocket, late June 1944. Wreckage of destroyed German equipment. Soviet troops inspect some captured vehicles, including a VW Schwimmwagen (left), a StuG IV assault gun (middle) and a staff car (right). (TsAMO)

When we entered Bobruisk some buildings in it were ablaze and others lay in ruins. To Bobruisk led the road of revenge! With difficulty, our car finds its way amid scorched and distorted German tanks and self-propelled guns. Men are walking over German corpses. Corpses, hundreds and thousands of them, pave the road, lie in ditches, under the pines, in the green barley. In some places, vehicles have to drive over the corpses, so densely they lie upon the ground. People are busy all the time burying them, but they are so many that this work cannot be done in just one day. And the day is exhaustingly hot, still, and people walk and

The Bobruisk pocket, late June 1944. Wreckage of destroyed German equipment. One can see a knocked-out Sd.Kfz. 7 prime mover with attached 8.8 cm Flak heavy anti-aircraft gun at the forefront. (TsAMO)

> drive pressing handkerchiefs to their noses. A cauldron of death was boiling here, where the revenge was carried out – a ruthless, terrible revenge over those who hadn't surrendered their arms and tried to break out to the west.
>
> A German soldier wounded in the legs is sitting on a low sandy bank of the Beresina by the route into the burning and destroyed Bobruisk. He raises his head and looks up at the tank columns moving across the bridge, at the artillery. A Red Army soldier comes up to him, takes some water from the river in a tin and gives it to him to drink. I couldn't help thinking, what would this German have done in the summer of 1941, when panzer columns of their troops were moving east across this bridge, if he had seen one of our soldiers with wounded legs sitting here on the sandy bank. [15]

The catastrophe at Bobruisk shook the German chain of command to the core. Thus, on 26 June *General der Infanterie* Hans Jordan was relieved of command of 9. Army. He was replaced by *General der Panzertruppe* Nikolaus von Vormann, an extremely capable staff officer and field commander, and a master of mobile warfare. Two days later *Feldmarschall* Ernst Busch was also sacked. His place was taken by Walter Model, Hitler's most celebrated "fireman".

By 29 June the bulk of the German 9. Army had been annihilated and Bobruisk had been completely cleared by the Soviets. A large gap, about 110 km wide, emerged in the very middle of the frontline of Army Group "Center". Rokossovsky didn't miss the chance to exploit the situation in his favor and pushed through the breach one of his most trusted mobile formations, the 1st Guards Tank Corps. There was nothing that could stop the brigades of Major-General Panov and on 3 July they reached Minsk where they established contact with the spearheads of the 3rd Byelorussian Front.

On the same day when Bobruisk was liberated, Rokossovsky's military talent was recognized again – he was promoted to Marshal of the Soviet Union, the highest military rank in the Red Army. Moreover, exactly a month later he was awarded both Hero of the Soviet Union golden star and Order of Lenin for his major contribution to the destruction of Army Group "Center" in Byelorussia.

15 Grossman, op. cit.

CHAPTER 5

PURSUIT TO THE WEST

TO MINSK AND BEYOND

On 28 June the Stavka ordered the 1st Byelorussian Front to advance on Minsk with some portion of his its forces, while with the bulk of its troops to strike towards Slutsk and Baranovichi, with the objective of cutting off the enemy's lines of retreat to the southwest. Subsequently, in conjunction with the armies of the 3rd Byelorussian Front approaching from the northeast, it was to effect a speedy encirclement of the German troops east of Minsk.

Rokossovsky immediately created two "shock" groups. The first one was made of 3rd Army of General Gorbatov and two tank corps (1st Guards and 9th); it was aimed at Minsk. The second one consisted of 28th and 65th Armies plus the Pliev Cavalry Mechanized Group. It was to advance on Slutsk and beyond, to Nesvizh. The 48th Army was to maintain the frontline between the two task forces.

As usual, the offensive of the task forces were spearheaded by mobile formations. Especially distinguishing themselves were the tankers and the cavalrymen of General Pliev. On the evening of 29 June they reached Slutsk where they encountered stiff resistance from the battle groups of two badly mauled German divisions (35. and 102.). Pliev was resolute in his intention to take the town without delay and decided to combine a pincer movement with direct attack. This worked out and by midday on 30 June Slutsk was taken after fierce street fighting.

Then Pliev rushed his troops back into action and in a matter of the next 48 hours they advanced about 90 km, facing only sporadic resistance in their path. On 2 July the tanks and the cavalry captured Nesvizh, a key town protecting the Minsk – Brest motorway and railroad. Thus, all likely supply routes running from Minsk to the southwest were blocked and the German troops still retreating towards the Byelorussian capital found themselves in a hopeless situation. The double envelopment was completed by the forces of the neighboring 3rd and 48th Armies. On 3 July the former, with the 1st Guards Tank Corps in the lead, reached Minsk, while the latter, closely cooperating with the 9th Tank Corps, secured the area of Pukhovichi. The German 12. Panzer-Division attempted to keep the friendly retreat paths open and even launched counterattacks, but was way too weak in numbers to stop the Red armored avalanche for good.

Gerd Niepold, then Ia (the chief of operations) officer of 12. Panzer-Division, recalls the importance of the counterattacks launched by the division:

> At dawn on 30 June Lapitschi again was attacked by strong Russian forces, supposedly from the small bridgehead taken on 29 June. A deep penetration was achieved. The panzer grenadier battalion at Talka also was under attack. Without delay the division launched a counterattack with the combined three panzer-grenadier battalions and the mass of the tank battalion across the military camp at Lapitschi. In severe fighting the enemy was slowly thrown back across the Svisloch River.
>
> At 1506 hours the CINC and Chief of Staff 9th Army telephoned to headquarters 12th Panzer Division. The CINC asked me: "Do you believe yourself capable of striking towards Svisloch town in order to relieve the Bobruisk garrison? The fate of 30,000 men depends on that!" The Chief of Staff suggested that we disengage

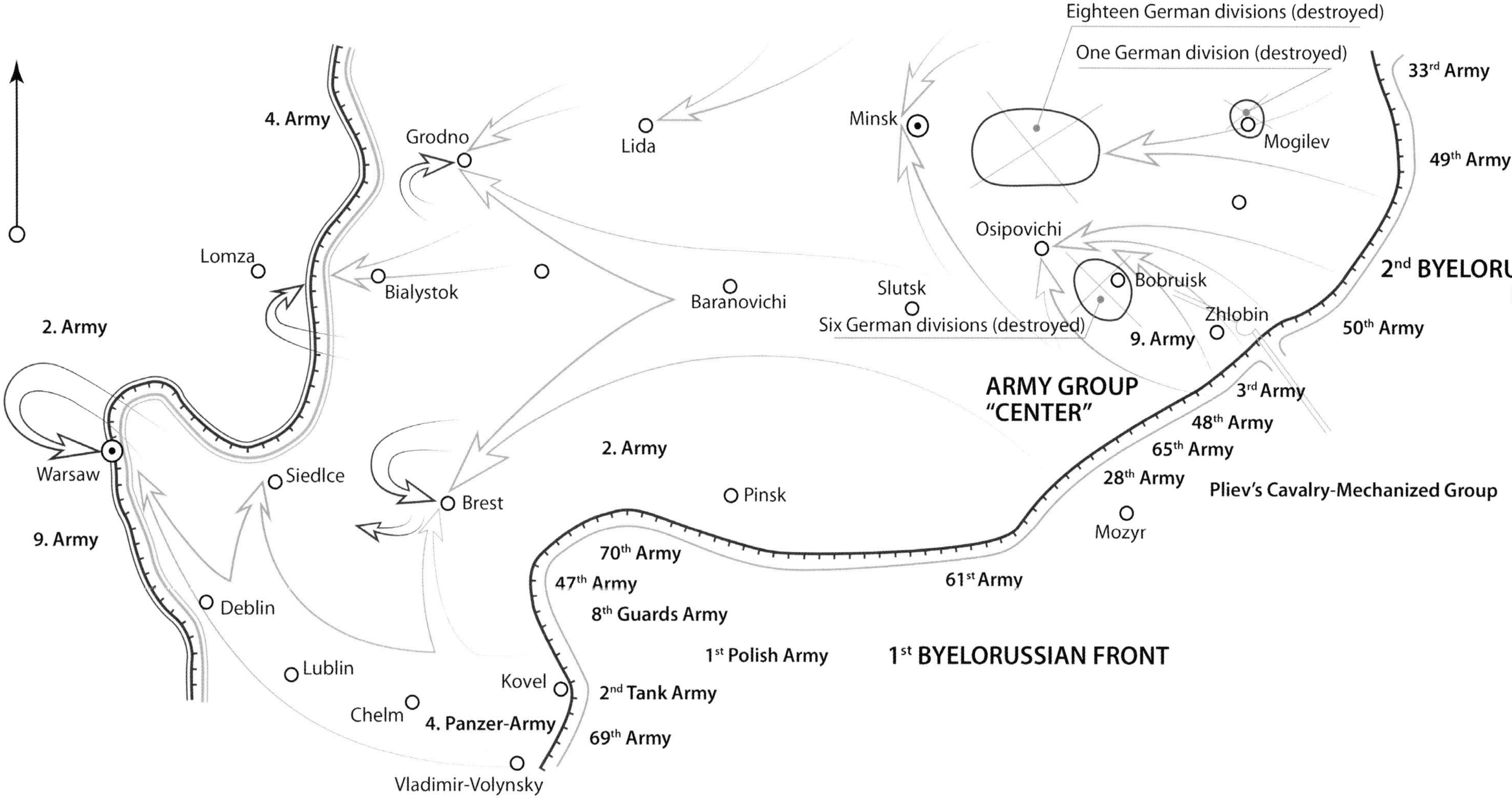
Eighteen German divisions (destroyed)
One German division (destroyed)
33rd Army
4. Army
Grodno
Lida
Minsk
Mogilev
49th Army
Lomza
Bialystok
Baranovichi
Slutsk
Osipovichi
Bobruisk
Zhlobin
Six German divisions (destroyed)
9. Army
2nd BYELORUSSIAN FRONT
50th Army
2. Army
ARMY GROUP "CENTER"
3rd Army
48th Army
65th Army
28th Army
Pliev's Cavalry-Mechanized Group
Mozyr
Warsaw
Siedlce
Brest
2. Army
Pinsk
9. Army
70th Army
47th Army
61st Army
Deblin
8th Guards Army
1st Polish Army
1st BYELORUSSIAN FRONT
Lublin
Kovel
2nd Tank Army
Chelm
4. Panzer-Army
69th Army
Vladimir-Volynsky

from the present attack. I refused this proposal, since we then would be unable to prevent the expected breakthrough towards Minsk tomorrow if today we did not succeed in repelling the enemy attacks across the Svisloch River.

At 1510 hours the CINC ordered 12th Panzer Division to launch a relief attack from Pogoreloje towards Svisloch on 1 July, if possible even before first light. The strength of the units to be committed was left to the division's estimate since only the division was capable of evaluating the situation. The division was to use the full extent of its power.

During the night of 30 June the division's achievement was obvious. Near Lapitschi the enemy had been repelled back across the Svisloch River, and around Talka the battalion had been able to hold its position by destroying ten enemy tanks. The report of General Panov was most interesting. He stated that his 17th [Guards] Tank Brigade had engaged us near Lapitschi, whilst his 15th and 16th [Guards] Tank Brigades as well as 1st Guards Rifle Brigade had thrust via Talka towards Marina Gorka. Shamefully, Panov passed over in silence the setback of 17th Tank Brigade at Lapitschi, which enabled us to make the relief attack towards Svisloch town. In the Talka area the mass of the Soviet tank corps obviously had not struck forcibly for our panzer grenadier battalion succeeded in holding its position.

During the night of 30 June /1 July we were able to begin our relief attack and decided to release from the endangered front no more than one panzer-grenadier battalion and a tank company. More was not feasible because if our defense at the Svisloch did not hold onto the river the Bobruisk forces would be lost even after their liberation.

During 1 July fortune smiled upon us! Early at night the mechanized panzer-grenadier battalion (minus one company, but plus one tank company) was concentrated near Ossovo and replenished. At 0210 hours the task force moved forward into action. At 0500 hours the Bobruisk force reported their position as being 3 kilometers south of the Svisloch River and west of the enemy held town of Svisloch.

The attack of the 12th Panzer Division task force reached Malinowka within 3 hours, a distance of 25 kilometers, without any contact with the enemy. Then, 5 kilometers to the southeast it was engaged with gradually increasing resistance which it fought until it reached about 2 kilometers in front of Svisloch town. There it was repulsed into a semi-circle position near Sapradje. Meanwhile, in the rear of the battalion 20,000 to 30,000 German soldiers from Bobruisk

Panther Ausf. A tanks of II. Battalion/SS-Panzer-Regiment 5 of 5. SS-Panzer-Division "Wiking" in action in the vicinity of Kovel. (Didier Laugier)

appeared out of the woods, without cohesion, disorganized, with many wounded and without weapons. It was a picture of misery! They were directed to Marina Gorka and moved back by waiting railway trains. The panzer grenadier battalion was repeatedly urged to hurry up. At 1830 hours it began its return and arrived early on 2 July near Puchowitschi. During the night of 1 to 2 July 12th Panzer Division withdrew behind the Zitovka River. This was the only successful relief attack during Operation "Bagration".

During this action 9th Army issued orders consciously according to *Auftragstaktik*. 12th Panzer Division had complete freedom of action and full choice of its own forces, although these were very limited. The panzer-grenadier task force also had full freedom of action to accomplish its mission.

Early in the morning on 3 July, 12th Panzer Division began its rearward movement south of Minsk to the Niemen River at Stolpce. At 0530 hours the Soviet spearhead entered the city of Minsk from the north. [16]

* * *

Immediately after the liberation of Minsk, Stalin ordered Rokossovsky to continue the pursuit of the remnants of the Army Group "Center" to the west, in the general direction of Brest. All forces of the right wing of the 1st Byelorussian Front were to be involved, save for Gorbatov's 3rd Army, which already had been placed under the neighboring 2nd Byelorussian Front. The immediate objective of the new offensive was the key junction town of Baranovichi, while Pinsk was to be taken not later than 10-12 July. Subsequently, Rokossovsky's armies were to capture Brest and secure bridgeheads on the far bank of the Western Bug.

Rokossovsky and his staff decided to destroy the enemy group defending Baranovichi by a series of pincer movements. For that purpose he gathered all his mobile formations there, namely the 9th Tank Corps, 1st Guards Tank Corps and Pliev's group. But *Feldmarschall* Model was under orders to defend the town at any cost and had already assembled in its vicinity the so-called Group *"Harteneck"*, the I. Cavalry Corps of *General der Kavallerie* Gustav Harteneck. It was made up of two division-sized German cavalry brigades, a Hungarian cavalry division and a German Jaeger (light-infantry) division. It also had one very powerful armored asset, the full-strength 4. Panzer-Division (about 180 tanks and tank-destroyers), which was

SS-Sturmbannführer Hubert-Erwin Meierdress (right), commander of I. Battalion/SS-Panzer-Regiment 3 of 3. SS-Panzer-Division "Totenkopf", in conversation with a member of the same division, probably a motorcycle messenger. A knocked-out T-34/85 of the Soviet 9th Tank Corps is in the background. The photo was taken in the last days of July 1944 in the vicinity of Siedlce. (NAC)

16 D. Glantz (Ed.), "1985 Art of War Symposium", Carlisle, US Army War College, 1985, pp. 436-438.

additionally reinforced with Heavy-Panzer-Battalion 507 (48 Tigers) and Assault-Gun Brigade 904 (31 StuG 40). A heavy battle ensued.

The fierce armored clashes at Baranovichi began on 5 July, when the spearheads of the 1st Mechanized Corps ran into some elements of 4. Panzer-Division. Soon more units joined in and the battle intensified. The Germans and the Magyars put up a tough resistance and the advance of the Soviets stalled. On the following day the situation remained unchanged and only Batov's 65th Army reported some progress.

Gradually, the Soviet superiority in numbers began to tell. The troops on the ground received considerable support from the friendly air force, the VVS. The Axis positions were repeatedly strafed by Shturmoviks and, in addition, were heavily pounded by about 500 bombers. Eventually, the German and Hungarian units gave way, and on 8 July the Soviet infantry penetrated into the town. It was completely secured by the end of the same day.

The account of Hans Schäufler perfectly summarizes the actions of 4. Panzer-Division in Southern Byelorussia during the period in question:

> We initially assembled in the southern sector of the Eastern Front. On 28 June, the first elements were taken to the central sector by rail to be committed against the Russian's large-scale offensive. The trip took four days, since partisans continuously blew up the rail lines.
>
> We were already being attacked by Russian fighter-bombers as we detrained. Schultz's battalion, which had been the first to arrive, was already committed and inflicted heavy blows to the enemy, together with the mechanized infantry.
>
> The days of fighting between 2 and 16 July can be summarized as follows: Hard defensive fighting. Those engagements, which took place during a series of withdrawal movements, were not the kind that you wanted to participate in as an armored division. It must be said, however, that the enemy did not succeed in breaking though at a single location where Panzer-Regiment 35 was used as a mobile fist. All of the efforts of the Russians to get past us failed, and we had the feeling that Ivan did not want to tangle too seriously with us. Unfortunately, he found opportunities far from our wings to break through, with the result that we also had to pull back again and again in order not to be cut off. This type of fighting often led to dramatic situations.
>
> While the withdrawal movements headed west, the regiment undertook an energetic thrust to the east. On 3 July, separated only by the run of a river, it linked up with a neighboring division. The division commander personally led the attack. Our return the next day forced us to negotiate a corridor 20 kilometers long but only 2 kilometers wide. The I./Panzer-Regiment 35 boxed its way out by attacking to the front, while the II./Panzer-Regiment 35 provided covering fire for the retrograde movements of the wheeled elements.
>
> The maintenance company had not been loaded out on trains initially. A sweet revenge was extracted for that later on. Although we had not suffered many combat losses, there were a lot of mechanical problems that could not be attended to in a professional manner right away. As a result, the number of operational vehicles shrunk rapidly. The maintenance contact sections and the recovery sections performed miracles. Tanks were recovered in the most unbelievable situations.
>
> There were also situations like that on 5 July, when the 1st Battalion had to move out for a decisive attack with only 20 vehicles. The 2nd Battalion had only 8. We had to stop the advance of the enemy along the southern wing of the division. Despite that, both of the battalions enjoyed great success. The Panthers knocked out more than 20 enemy tanks. The 2nd Battalion, with only four main guns firing in the end, advanced against a road nodal point that was heavily defended and took it. The successful resistance offered at Baranowitschi and Slonim that was extolled in the Armed Forces Daily Report was thanks to the 4. Panzer-Division.
>
> Kampfgruppe Christern—Panzer-Regiment 35, Panzeraufklärungs-Abteilung 4, an SPW battalion, an artillery battalion and a company of engineers—became the mobile fire brigade. Wherever things were hot, it was employed as an iron fist. The coordination and cooperation within the battle group was extraordinary. The armored raiding parties defeated all enemy attacks. The artillery went into positions next to an ammo dump and fired with everything they had. They only paused from firing when the barrels turned glowing hot.
>
> The supply sections had to give their all during that fighting in order to have ammunition and fuel where it was needed. The operational tanks fought in the south … then in the north … wherever the enemy was hoping for a success.
>
> Once again, withdrawal movements were initiated by the armored battle group first thrusting into the enemy. He then tried to go around us in the large, marshy wooded terrain. But Kampfgruppe Christern was employed in time in the deep flank, with the result that the planned actions on the German side were not disturbed. We even had the opportunity to sleep occasionally. We were also "loaned out" to the neighboring divisions on occasion.

In the meantime, we also got our maintenance facility back. In the blink of an eye, an amazing amount of repaired tanks returned to the regiment. Hauptmann Schaeffer remained with his troops to convalesce from his wounds.
The mission of the division — prevent the front from being torn open — was accomplished. A new defensive line was established. Fresh divisions were brought forward. [17]

AFV LOSSES OF THE FORMATIONS OF THE RIGHT WING OF 1ST BYELORUSSIAN FRONT,
24 June – 17 July 1944

3rd Army: All losses (including AFVs in workshops) – 118 tanks and 137 SP guns; total write-offs - 33 tanks and 50 SP guns

28th Army: All losses (including AFVs in workshops) – 199 tanks and 129 SP guns; total write-offs - 42 tanks and 29 SP guns

48th Army: All losses (including AFVs in workshops) – 94 tanks and 88 SP guns; total write-offs - 16 tanks and 16 SP guns

65th Army: All losses (including AFVs in workshops) – 203 tanks and 68 SP guns; total write-offs - 10 tanks and 17 SP guns

4th Guards Cavalry Corps: All losses (including AFVs in workshops) – 74 tanks and 23 SP guns; total write-offs - 6 tanks and 7 SP guns

1st Guards Tank Corps: All losses (including AFVs in workshops) – 387 tanks and 83 SP guns; total write-offs - 122 tanks and 17 SP guns

9th Tank Corps: All losses (including AFVs in workshops) – 411 tanks and 98 SP guns; total write-offs - 84 tanks and 9 SP guns

1st Mechanized Corps: All losses (including AFVs in workshops) – 354 tanks and 78 SP guns; total write-offs - 74 tanks and 18 SP guns

17 Schäufler, "Knight's Cross Panzers".

A German Sd.Kfz. 10/4 self-propelled gun (a 2 cm Flak 38 auto-cannon mounted on a half-track) employed in ground-combat role on the bank of the Vistula, August 1944. (NAC)

* * *

The victory at Baranovichi also speeded up the clearing of the Pripet Marshes. It was carried out by General Belov's 61st Army, which had remained inactive throughout the Bobruisk Operation. Hopes were high that his divisions would be able to block the retreat of Group *"Harteneck"* from Baranovichi by a daring pincer movement, but the advance of the troops was largely delayed by the forests, swamps and marshy terrain. On top of that the German 2. Army conducted a very skillful fighting withdrawal, thereby making any entrapment an impossible accomplishment.

Overcoming all difficulties, Belov's men kept going forward. On 10 July they captured the town of Luninets and approached Pinsk, the biggest settlement in the area. Then the Dnieper Flotilla joined the pursuit. The gunboats sailed up the Pripet and landed a whole rifle regiment at Pinsk. The Germans failed to eliminate the bridgehead and on 14 July the town fell into Soviet hands. Wasting no time, the advance detachments of the 61st Army continued their raid to the west and on 19 July began to envelop Kobrin, the last big town before Brest. It was taken by storm on the next day by two divisions of the army's 9th Guards Rifle Corps. Immediately afterwards the 61st Army disengaged and was withdrawn into reserve.

THE DISASTER AT KOVEL

The battle of Baranovichi had just begun when Rokossovsky decided to bring into play his powerful left wing. The "shock" group was to launch a sharp pincer attack from the vicinity of Kovel, swing to the north and cut off the retreat paths of the German 2. Army. His decision was fueled up by the withdrawal of the Germans from Kovel that took place during the night of 4/5 July. The recently promoted Marshal immediately ordered the 47th Army to take the town. During the day the assault units of General Gusev penetrated into the town and on the next day completely secured it.

On 6 July the offensive of the 1st Byelorussian Front intensified. Not only 69th Army joined the battle, but also the full-strength 11th Tank Corps (Major-General Philip Rudkin) was placed under the 47th Army. The mission of Rudkin's corps was, by driving deep into the German rear, to secure a bridgehead on the western bank of the Bug. Subsequently it was to advance on Lublin.

The 11th Tank Corps entered the battle at midday on 8 July. The attack was poorly prepared and before long the leading two brigades were ambushed by the Panthers of 5. SS-Panzer-Division *"Wiking"* and sustained heavy losses: 82 T-34s became total write-offs. The corps was immediately pulled out of combat and soon Rudkin was relieved of command. The offensive in the vicinity of Kovel was called off, too.

A member of the *"Wiking"* Panther Battalion, SS-Obersturmführer Lichte, who was also among the participants in the fighting at Kovel, provides a vivid account of the engagement:

> The enemy did not notice the withdrawal movements — at least, that's what we thought — and everything proceeded without incident during the cover of the night. At first light, the battalion staff set up operations with its three tanks and the communications section in a farmstead on the east side of Maciejow.
> To celebrate the successful action — it was a brilliant Sunday morning — the adjutant and the liaison officer decided to do some general personal hygiene after living in the woods without suitable sanitary facilities. A former Soviet soldier, whom we picked up somewhere and had incorporated into the ranks of the communications section, got a few buckets of water. "Ivan" —that's what everyone called him — was a jack-of-all-trades. He was an excellent cook; he was coldblooded and resourceful in finding breaks in the wires; and, when things turned hot, he always grabbed a rifle so as not to have to trade sides once again.
> The twin pillars of the headquarters first turned to their beards. The ritual was disturbed in a most unfriendly way by a low-level air attack that was delivered with an intensity hitherto unknown. After the roof of the house caught fire, the adjutant and the liaison officer, clothed only in swimming trunks, excused themselves to a tank dugout outside of the house door, pulling along a field telephone. After cranking it a bit, both of them determined that the wires to the companies had been cut. Since strong artillery fire had commenced in the meantime, it was clear what the culprit was. Ivan, our friend and Hiwi, jumped out into the heavy fire to find the break.
> All of a sudden, the two warriors in their swimming trunks heard the sound of engines. The unforgettable liaison officer, Untersturmführer Jensen, who hailed from Holstein and was well known for his non-flappable nature, asked the adjutant: "What kind of idiot is driving around in this type of artillery fire?".
> They lifted their noses over the edge of the dugout and saw three full-fledged T-34's only 50 meters away. The tank commanders were standing in their cupolas and observing. Thank god, it was in the wrong direction. The adjutant and the liaison officer jumped into a nearby well-camouflaged Panther in their non-regulation uniforms and knocked out two T-34's. The [battalion] commander took on the third one at just that moment. At that short of a distance, all of the Ivans literally flew into the air.
> It goes without saying that all of the companies launched [an immediate] counterattack without waiting for orders. The engagement that developed under the leadership of the battalion commander, Hauptsturmführer Reichert, proved to be a high point in the history of the Panther battalion. First off, the T-34's that were romping around in the firing positions of the artillery were nailed. Then our own front lines were reached. The reverse-slope position that we occupied was so ideal that tactics instructors at Wünsdorf could not have invented a better one. Despite that, the enemy assaulted for two days continuously with new waves of tanks and lost a total of 99 T-34's and T-43's, without one Panther being a total write-off.
> Whatever caused the commander on the opposite side to run into the same trap again and again and lose nearly all of his regiment in the process will always remain incomprehensible to someone who understands something about tanking.

In a summary of the fighting from 6–10 July in the area between Kowel and Maciejow, the Armed Forces Daily Report of 11 July announced:

In the area around Kowel, forces of the Army and the Waffen-SS have turned back the assault of 10 rifle divisions, a tank corps and two tank brigades in four days of

A German Pz IV Ausf. J of 5. Company/Panzer-Regiment 27 of 19. Panzer-Division and a Sd.Kfz. 251/3 command-post armored halftrack during one of the many desperate German attempts to smash the Magnuszew bridgehead. The photo probably was taken at the village of Studzianki, August 1944. (NAC)

hard defensive fighting. In the process, they inflicted considerable losses in men and materiel. During the fighting, 295 enemy armored vehicles were destroyed at the front and in the rear area by the combined effects of all weapons.
The 342. Infanterie-Division, from the Rhine and Mosel area and under the command of Generalmajor Nickel, the 26. Infanterie-Division, from the Rhine and Westphalia area and under the [acting] command of Oberst Frommberger, and a battle group from the 5. SS-Panzer-Division Wiking, under the command of SS-Standartenführer Mühlenkamp, distinguished themselves through their exemplary bravery. [18]

JANÓW PODLASKI AND KLESZCZELE: TWO MORE TRAPS

After the securing the area of Baranovichi the right wing of Rokossovsky's Front (48th, 28th and 65th Armies) pushed forward as rapidly as possible. It was spearhead by Pliev's cavalry-mechanized group, which now combined all mobile formations operating in that area, namely the 4th Guards Cavalry Corps, 1st Mechanized Corps and 9th Tank Corps, while the 1st Guards Tank Corps was pulled out of action for reconstitution, because it already had lost most of its armor.

The ultimate objective of the Front's right wing was the taking of Brest and its vicinity, as well the annihilation of the German troops defending that area. The decisive blow was to be delivered by the Pliev Group, which was to cut off the rear communications by a daring pincer attack.

From 11 to 15 July Pliev's group actively pursued the defeated troops of Weiss' 2. Army, giving them no chance to make a stand. On 17 July the tankers and the cavalrymen severed the Białystok – Brest railway, but then the German resistance dramatically increased. General Weiss proved once again that he knew pretty well how to handle critical situations.

On 18 July Pliev's spearheads crossed the Bug at Janów Podlaski, just northwest of Brest, but almost immediately were counterattacked by elements of 5. SS-Panzer-Division *"Wiking"* and 3. Cavalry Brigade and were surrounded. Five days of extremely heavy fighting followed before the Soviets eventually managed to break out of the trap.

Further to the northwest, at Kleszczele, Weiss managed to encircle yet another Soviet spearhead, that of Batov's 65th Army. On 21 July Batov's forward detachments reached the Bug somewhere southwest of Kleszczele, but two days later their weakly protected flanks were counterattacked by 4. Panzer-Division and 5. SS-Panzer-Division from the northwest and southwest, respectively. Part of Batov's army found itself caught in a trap and only the timely arrival of some reserves dispatched by Rokossovsky (including a tank brigade of 1st Guards Tank Corps) saved him from great trouble.

A commander of one of the staff companies of the *"Wiking"* panzer-regiment gives more details on an engagement between a Flak platoon and an unknown Soviet unit that took place at Czeremcha, not far from Kleszczele, on 25 July:

> In position around Czeremcha and the woods west of Czeremcha. Around 1000 hours, breakthrough of the Russians in the eastern part of Czeremcha. Decisive defensive efforts on the part of the two guns of the Flak platoon. Old main line of resistance re-established.
> Towards 1700 hours, I saw friendly infantry pull back. The sounds of fighting coming from the west out of the woods. A noncommissioned officer from the Westland [SS-Panzer-Grenadier-Regiment] command post reported that a quad Flak needed to be sent forward. The Russians were going to attack with strong forces.
> No. 2 gun moved to the main line of resistance and opened fire against the wood line. All of a sudden, 12 T-34's came out of the woods. At the same time, orders arrived for the battalion to pull both of the guns back, since the guns were defenseless against tanks. By order of the battalion commander of the 1st Battalion of Westland, the guns remained in position, however, and attempted to escape the tanks, some of which were moving past, by continuing evasive maneuvers by the prime movers.
> Two of the T-34's were knocked out by the 14th Company of Westland. One of the antitank guns of the 14th Company then received a direct hit and was disabled. Gun No. 1 succeeded in knocking out two 7.62-centimeter antitank guns and separating the infantry from the tanks, causing them to suffer heavy casualties. As a result, the Russians were only able to enter Czeremcha with their tanks. Later on, they lost all of their tanks when they entered the kill zone of our tanks and the 8th Company advanced with its Panthers. Both of the guns were pulled back, since they had accomplished their mission. One man received a stomach wound, but he remained with his gun. At night, the old positions were reoccupied. [19]

18 E. Klapdor, "Viking Panzers", Mechanicsburg, Stackpole Books, 2011, pp. 278-279.

19 Klapdor, op. cit., pp. 316-317.

CHAPTER 6

THE BATTLE AT THE GATES OF WARSAW

THE LUBLIN – BREST OFFENSIVE

On 18 July the left wing of the 1st Byelorussian Front finally launched its long-anticipated offensive from the vicinity of Kovel. Now Rokossovsky was at last able to commit to battle all his armies. This was very bad news for *Feldmarschall* Model, who already had spent all his reserves and had nothing on hand with which to check the new Soviet onslaught. Now he had no other choice left, but to pull back the 4. Panzer-Army, which had been caught between Scylla and Charybdis (i.e. between Rokossovsky and Konev) and was in danger of being completely annihilated.

The Soviet 8th Guards and 47th Armies surged forward at great speed and on 21 July crossed the Bug on a broad front. The German VIII. Army Corps not only failed to occupy the defensive positions on the western riverbank, but disintegrated in no time and now yet another dangerous gap emerged in the middle of the Ostfront. Rokossovsky didn't miss the chance to exploit the situation and immediately committed to battle two very powerful mobile formations: the 2nd Tank Army of Colonel-General Bogdanov and the Cavalry-Tank Group of General Baranov (2nd Guards Cavalry Corps and 11th Tank Corps). The former rapidly advanced to the west, in the direction of Lublin, while the latter was turned to the north/northwest, towards Brest.

It was at Brest that the forces of the 1st Byelorussian Front managed to set up one more trap for the retreating Germans. On 25 July the spearheads of the 70th and 65th Armies met to the west of the town and three divisions of Weiss' 2. Army were caught in a cauldron. Three days later their remnants managed to breakout to the west, but this was achieved at the cost of heavy losses. (After clearing the area, the Soviets claimed to have counted about 7,000 dead bodies on the battlefield. On the other hand, they reported a very small number of POWs – no more than 110 men.)

The German casualties would have been much higher without the timely intervention of some elements of 3. SS-Panzer-Division *"Totenkopf"*, and especially of the newly formed battalion of Panther tanks, which had just arrived from France. Martin Steiger, the company commander of 1./SS-Panzer-Regiment 3, recalls the rescue mission:

> Our transport arrived in Warsaw without difficulties. It was already midnight when we began the unloading. The rest of the Abteilung also arrived during this night and was again incorporated into the "T" Division. The division had been in action without a break for a full year and was urgently expecting the new "Panther-Abteilung." Battle orders to the Abteilung were issued around midnight of the next day.
>
> We had to get to Siedlce as quickly as possible. There, a strong thrust by the Russians threatened to break through the German lines protruding to the east. It was about eighty kilometers from Warsaw to Siedlce. We rolled just after noon, in burning heat, and reached the edge of the city of Siedlce around 3 P.M. What we saw during this race to the front describes the situation more accurately than the most detailed report. Fleeing soldiers, female communications operators, civilian workers of the "Organisation Todt," and railway personnel crowded the retreat route. Some of the shouts from the masses flooding backward hit us

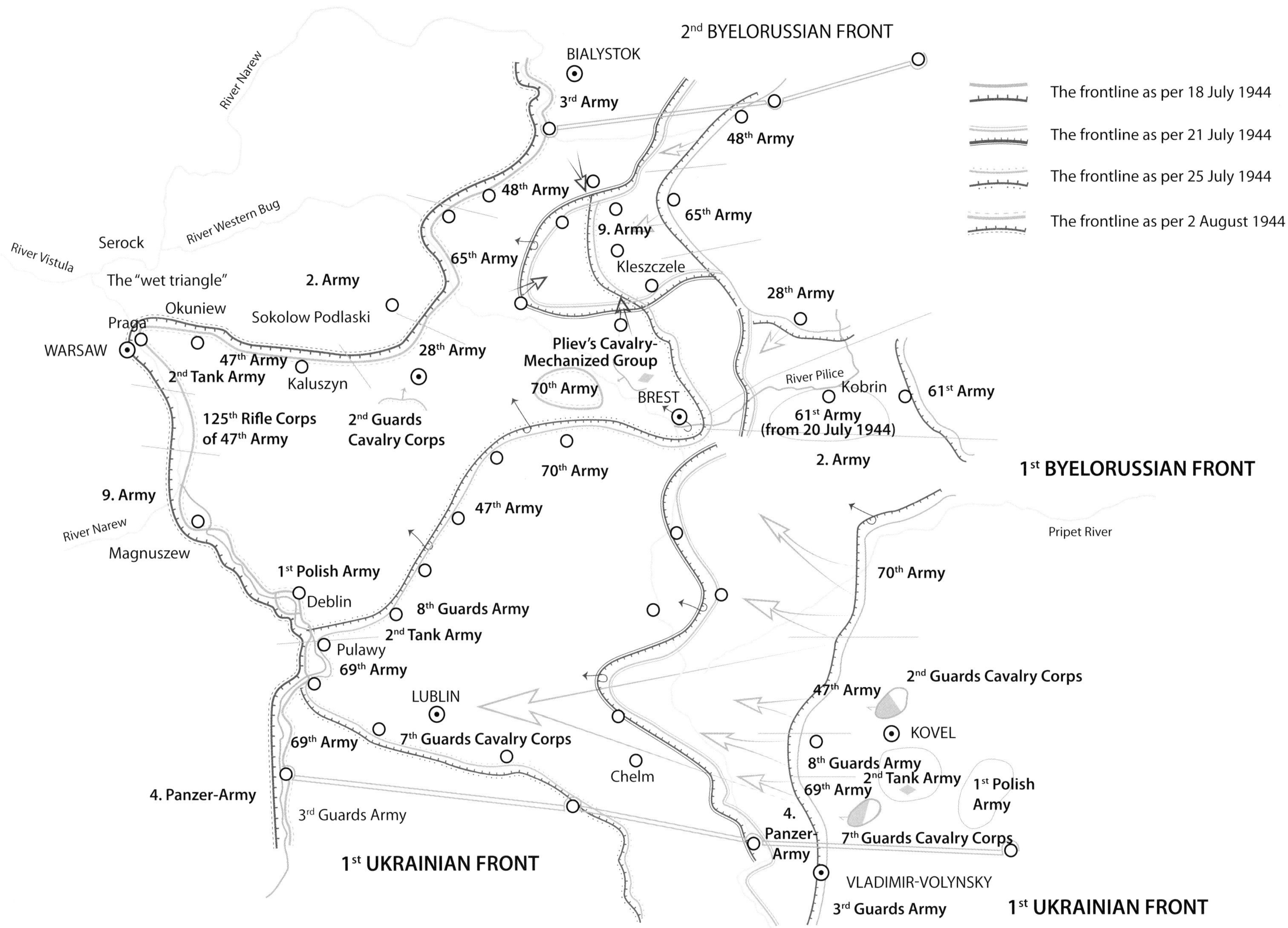
2nd BYELORUSSIAN FRONT
The frontline as per 18 July 1944
The frontline as per 21 July 1944
The frontline as per 25 July 1944
The frontline as per 2 August 1944
BIALYSTOK
3rd Army
48th Army
River Narew
48th Army
65th Army
9. Army
River Western Bug
Serock
River Vistula
Kleszczele
65th Army
The "wet triangle"
2. Army
28th Army
Okuniew
Sokolow Podlaski
Praga
Pliev's Cavalry-Mechanized Group
WARSAW
47th Army
28th Army
2nd Tank Army
Kaluszyn
70th Army
River Pilice
Kobrin
61st Army
BREST
61st Army (from 20 July 1944)
125th Rifle Corps of 47th Army
2nd Guards Cavalry Corps
70th Army
2. Army
1st BYELORUSSIAN FRONT
9. Army
47th Army
River Narew
Pripet River
Magnuszew
70th Army
1st Polish Army
Deblin
8th Guards Army
2nd Tank Army
Pulawy
69th Army
2nd Guards Cavalry Corps
LUBLIN
47th Army
KOVEL
69th Army
7th Guards Cavalry Corps
8th Guards Army
Chelm
2nd Tank Army
1st Polish Army
69th Army
4. Panzer-Army
3rd Guards Army
4. Panzer-Army
7th Guards Cavalry Corps
1st UKRAINIAN FRONT
VLADIMIR-VOLYNSKY
3rd Guards Army
1st UKRAINIAN FRONT

SS-Obersturmführer Karl Nicolussi-Leck, commander of 8. Company/SS-Panzer-Regiment 5 of 5. SS-Panzer-Division "Wiking" (second from the left) stands between his tank (the '800' Panther Ausf. A) and the Sd.Kfz. 251/3 Ausf. D command-post halftrack, the Warsaw area, August 1944. (NAC)

A StuG III Ausf. G of Panzer-Battalion (radio-controlled) 302 in front of the Saxon Palace in Warsaw, August 1944. The battalion was equipped with Borgward B IV radio-controlled demolition vehicles, which purpose was to deliver explosives to the target that would be detonated remotely. To control the remote vehicles, assault guns were issued to the battalion for control and command. (Following the suppression of the Warsaw Uprising, the Saxon Palace was blown up by the Germans as part of their planned destruction of the Polish capital.) (NAC)

An SS tank commander, presumably of 5. SS-Panzer-Division "Wiking", inside a Panther tank, the Warsaw area, September 1944. Note the T.S.R.1 Sehstab, a thin periscope about 1.5 m long, mounted in the adjustable socket inside the cupola, which allowed the tank commander to reconnoiter the battlefield from turret-down position. (NAC)

like whips: "Warmongers — we're going home — we've had enough." Others, however, were more encouraging: "Drive them back, the Russians ..." etc. As we rolled into the center of the city, heavy Russian artillery fire came down as a greeting to welcome us. The city appeared to have already been deserted by German soldiers. Enemy tanks were reported.

We halted in the town center, and the platoon leaders were called to the chief of the company. Orders were issued:

"A German Army staff is encircled in Brest-Litowsk, our mission is to free them. The Abteilung, with the 1. Company at the point, will advance in a southeasterly direction at 8 P.M. Obersturmführer Schramm will command the point platoon; Oberscharführer Ober will be in the point vehicle. The enemy is holding positions with strong forces behind the railroad line."

We had barely crossed the railroad line at dusk when, at very close distance, destructive defensive firing started. The lead Panzer was knocked out, while two T-34s were also left burning on the road. Chaos seemed to set in. In the bright light of the burning tanks, we were clearly visible targets. The leader of the 2. Platoon, Untersturmführer von Rennenkampf, was critically wounded when he left his Panzer, as were some commanders and crew. The attack had failed; we had to return to Siedlce. A breakthrough succeeded only during the next day via Mordy to Losice, with heavy losses. Oberscharführer Kessler's crew was reported missing. Unterscharführer Massarei and Sturmmann Koser were killed, and Sturmmann Robel was killed by a shell fragment while under his Panzer in Siedlce. When we joined up again with the company three days later, the noncom in charge had the sad duty to write off a large part of the company as dead, missing, or wounded. On July 28, our chief was given the office of tank defense commander of the almost-lost city of Siedlce. During the afternoon of the same day, the sad news reached us that Riefkogel had been critically wounded by a grenade fragment and died a few hours later at the main field dressing station. His noncom in charge, who had still seen him alive there, conveyed his last words to the company:

"Take my greetings to my proud company. Obersturmführer Schramm is to lead it from now on in my spirit.". [20]

AFV STRENGTH OF THE SOVIET FORMATIONS OF THE LEFT WING OF 1ST BYELORUSSIAN FRONT,
23 June 1944

2nd Tank Army: 687 tanks and 126 SP guns
11th Tank Corps: 248 tanks and 42 SP guns
2nd Guards Cavalry Corps: 67 tanks and 22 SP guns
7th Guards Cavalry Corps: 60 tanks and 12 SP guns
47th Army: 73 tanks and 105 SP guns
8th Guards Army: 65 tanks
69th Army: 116 SP guns
1st Polish Army: 86 tanks and 86 SP guns

20 W. Fey, "Armor Battles of the Waffen SS 1943-45", Winnipeg, J.J. Fedorowicz Publishing, 1996, p. 106.

* * *

While the attention of Model and his staff was preoccupied with the crisis at Brest, Rokossovsky unleashed his main exploitation force, the super-strong 2nd Tank Army. It entered the battle in the early hours of 22 July and immediately advanced on Lublin. The taking of the latter was of high political importance to Stalin. At that time the principal Polish authority in German-occupied Poland was *Armia Krajowa*, an underground resistance movement that was directed by the government-in-exile based in London. But the Kremlin dictator wanted the country only for himself and once the Red Army crossed the 1941 border, Stalin proceeded with setting up a rival executive authority, one that he could control. It was abbreviated PKWN (*Polski Komitet Wyzwolenia Narodowego* or Polish Committee of National Liberation) dominated by the Polish communists and initially was seated in Chełm. The latter, however, was way too small even for a temporary capital and Stalin set his eyes on Lublin.

Not aware of Stalin's political machinations, on the morning of 22 July the tankers of Bogdanov's mighty army delivered a heavy blow on the retreating Germans. The leading formation, the 3rd Tank Corps, sliced the defense of VIII. Army Corps and began to outflank Lublin to the north. By the evening the corps not only had reached the northwestern outskirts of the town, but also had cut off the Puławy – Lublin motorway. Several German rear-area and administrative units fleeing from Lublin were suddenly attacked by the Soviet forward detachments. Lublin itself, however, proved to be a hard nut to crack. It was protected by earthworks (two concentric defensive belts) built in a hurry on orders of the city commandant. Moreover, many solid buildings had been fortified and transformed into strongpoints.

The signalmen of one of the batteries of the 40th Anti-Tank Artillery Brigade, the Warsaw area, 10 August 1944. The soldier in the left is armed with a Mosin–Nagant M1938 rifle, the one in the right – with a PPSh-41 submachine-gun. (TsAMO)

Having realized that Lublin could not be taken from the march, General Bogdanov ordered an all-out assault. The offensive began on the following morning. At first, the attacks of the brigades proceeded well and the suburbs were cleared quite quickly. But once the Soviets reached the downtown their thrust was checked by the defenders. It became obvious that the assault detachments formed by the tank army were critically short of infantry. At that difficult moment, they received unexpected help from *Armia Krajowa*. The Polish underground fighters launched a rebellion and the German resistance lessened. On the morning of 24 July the garrison began to leave the city, but not all of the defenders managed to escape. At midday the Soviet and Polish detachments reached the centre of the place and Lublin was officially declared liberated by the Red Army. Two days later PKWN made the city its official residence and before long it became known as the Lublin Committee.

The Soviets reported that the enemy garrison had been decimated. 2,228 prisoners were taken, including the city commandant, *SS-Gruppenführer* Hilmar Moser. The losses of the 2nd Tank Army were rather light. The army, however, sustained an unexpected blow: Colonel-General Bogdanov was heavily wounded on the afternoon of 23 July. His place was taken by Major-General Alexei Radzievsky, the army's chief-of-staff.

* * *

The spectacular success of the 1st Byelorussian Front surprised not only the Germans, but also the Soviet Supreme Command – according to the preliminary plans of the General Staff, the city was to be taken by 27 July. Neither Stalin, nor Rokossovsky wanted to lose the momentum gained so far and the 2nd Tank Army once again rolled to the west.

On 25 July Radzievsky's spearheads reached the Vistula, capturing two towns situated on the riverbank: Puławy and Dęblin. Then the tank army made a sharp turn to the north and advanced at a rapid pace to the Polish capital. Its three tank corps were in a very privileged situation: they surged forward without worrying about the safety of their flanks, because the western wing of the army was protected by the river and there was no enemy whatsoever to the east.

It didn't take Model long to realize that the main objective of the offensive of the 1st Byelorussian Front was Warsaw. That's why he urgently positioned the arriving reserves – 73. Infantry Division and the "Hermann Goering" Parachute-Panzer-Division - in the path of Radzievsky's forward detachments. Unfortunately for the Germans, both formations had to be committed piecemeal, in order of their arrival, over the span of several days. Worse still, their men performed poorly on the battlefield and were quickly defeated.

Both divisions had something in common – they had been recently reconstituted. The 73rd, in particular, had been badly mauled in Crimea in May 1944 and had been fully rebuilt in Hungary afterwards. The "Hermann Goering", on the other hand, had fought quite well in Tunisia and Italy, but it had never operated on the Eastern Front and lacked experience in fighting the Red Army. While en route to Warsaw, it was issued with nearly 100 tanks and tank-destroyers. In July and August it also received more than 3,000 manpower replacements, but nearly all of them were green Luftwaffe recruits and volunteers. Not surprisingly, the attempts of both divisions to establish a security line between Siedlce and the Vistula ended up in total failure: the forward parties of the "Hermann Goering" were defeated at the southern approaches to Kaluszyn, while elements of the 73rd were routed to the southwest of Okuniew. The commander of the latter, Generalleutnant Dr. Fritz Franek, was taken prisoner by the Soviets.

* * *

One of the formations of the 1st Byelorussian Front that experienced serious difficulties in the last week of July was the cavalry-tank group of General Baranov. It was under orders to swing to the northwest and block the retreat routes of the German forces trying to escape the Brest cauldron. Much to their bad luck, they ran into some of the most dreadful military formations, the fearsome SS-Panzer Divisions *"Wiking"* and *"Totenkopf"*.

The 11th Tank Corps and the 2nd Guards Cavalry Corps attempted to take Siedlce, a key junction town halfway between Warsaw and Brest, by attacking it simultaneously from south and east. The Waffen-SS, however, put up fanatical resistance and the

The crew of one of the 76-mm ZiS-3 guns of the 40th Anti-Tank Artillery Brigade is having a break, the Warsaw area, 11 August 1944. (TsAMO)

Troops of the 40th Anti-Tank Artillery Brigade inspect a knocked out German Sd.Kfz. 251 Ausf. D armored halftrack, the Warsaw area, 11 August 1944. The soldier at the forefront is armed with a Mosin–Nagant M1938 rifle (TsAMO)

A battery of the 40th Anti-Tank Artillery Brigade moves through a heavily damaged Polish village, the Warsaw area, 12 August 1944. The 76-mm ZiS-3 guns are towed by three-axle Lend-Lease trucks. (TsAMO)

town fell in Soviet hands only on 29 July, following some very heavy street fighting. Then the Germans gradually retreated to the west, not allowing the Soviets to break out into open country.

A commander of one the Tigers of SS-Panzer-Regiment 3 recorded the following about the fighting in the Siedlce area on 31 July 1944:

> Our Tiger turns on the spot and fires toward the end of the street. On our right is a rail embankment and behind that is the road leading to Chodow. The cannon fires an 8.8 cm shell from the barrel. The turret is full of smoke, so we leave the hatches open to allow the fumes to ventilate. Behind me is SS-Unterscharführer Holtorf, who hits a third Russian tank with a single shot. It catches fire. The crew bail out." [21]

21 I. M. Wood, "Tigers of the Death's Head", Mechanicsburg, Stackpole Books, 2013.

* * *

Excited by the spectacular success of Rokossovsky in Central Poland, during the night of 28/29 July Stalin assigned new, ambitious objectives to the 1st Byelorussian Front:

- Upon securing of the Brest - Siedlce area, the right wing of the Front was to attack in the general direction of Warsaw and not later than 5-8 August to capture Praga, as well to seize bridgeheads on the western bank of the Narew in the vicinity of Pułtusk and Serock.
- The left wing of the Front was to secure bridgeheads on the western bank of the Vistula at Dęblin, Zwoleń and Solec. Then the armies were to attack from these bridgeheads to the northwest with the aim of rolling back the enemy defensive lines along the Vistula and the Narew, as well as assisting the forces of the left wing of the 2nd Byelorussian Front in advancing forward.
- Subsequently, both wings of the Front were to strike to the northwest, towards Thorn and Łódź, respectively.

PUŁAWY AND MAGNUSZEW BRIDGEHEADS

The first Soviet formation that secured bridgeheads on the far side of the Vistula was the 69th Army of Lieutenant-General Kolpakchi. It was positioned on Rokossovsky's extreme left flank and fully benefited from the rapid breakthrough of the mighty 2nd Tank Army in the Lublin area. On 26 July Kolpakchi's troops captured the town of Krasnystaw and on the next day they reached the Vistula at Puławy.

The crossing of the river was carried out during the night of 28/29 July and by the morning three small bridgeheads were secured on the western bank. During the following thirty days they gradually enlarged and by the end of August consolidated into one large (134 km^2) foothold.

The establishing of the Puławy bridgehead is often described in the pro-Soviet literature as a great defensive success, but this was not exactly the case. It is often forgotten that, first and foremost, it was an offensive operation aimed at Łódź and the resolute German counterattacks ruined to a considerable degree the ambitious plans of the Stavka to capture Poland already during the summer of the 1944.

Speaking of which, the German reaction to the forced crossing of Kolpakchi's army was swift. From 1 to 6 August they transferred to the endangered zone 17.

Infantry Division (which had arrived from Rumania), SS-Police-Regiment 11 and elements of three other infantry divisions. The grenadiers and the policemen launched a series of resolute counterattacks supported by heavy artillery and assault guns, and eventually brought the offensive of the 69th Army to a standstill.

There is no doubt that Rokossovsky and his staff were unpleasantly surprised by the very slow expansion of the Puławy bridgehead. They intended to attack from there with the 11th Tank Corps, which on 1 August was assigned to the 69th Army. But the corps was ferried across the Vistula quite slowly, literally one unit at a time and it was not before 18 August that the brigades were transferred to the opposite bank. There they were used either to back up the anti-tank defense or as close support to some of the friendly rifle divisions.

Soviet troops inspect a StuG III Ausf. G assault gun knocked out by the 1956th Anti-Tank Artillery Regiment (40th Anti-Tank Artillery Brigade) in the vicinity of Stanisławów (east of Warsaw), the beginning of August 1944. The machine most probably had belonged to SS-Panzer-Regiment 5 of 5. SS-Panzer-Division "Wiking". Note the patch for anti-tank artillery on the sleeve of the officer at the forefront. (TsAMO)

* * *

The 8th Guards Army of Colonel-General Vasily Chuikov, the hero of Stalingrad, reached the Vistula at Magnuszew in the last days of July. Their sudden appearance at the southern approaches of Warsaw caught the Germans completely by surprise – it turned out that not a single Axis soldier had remained in that area and Chuikov's Guardsmen got an unexpected rest. (They spent the afternoon of 31July in taking baths in the river.)

The forced crossing of the Vistula began on 1 August, way ahead of the schedule, which called for the offensive to start on 4 August. Initially, the Germans, who had almost no troops in the area, attempted to disrupt the Soviet buildup by heavy artillery barrages. But once they realized that this was not going to halt the enemy, strong ground forces were moved to the endangered area, including the "Hermann Goering" Panzer-Division and 19. Panzer-Division. Rokossovsky, in turn, also moved more troops to the western bank – the 1st Polish Army and then the 16th Tank Corps of the temporarily disbanded 2nd Tank Army. A very savage seesaw battle ensued that lasted till the end of the month. The Soviets and Poles attempted to breakout to the west, but were stopped dead in their tracks by unceasing German counterattacks. On the other hand, the desperate attempts of the panzers and grenadiers to push the two armies into the Vistula were also unsuccessful. The struggle ended up in stalemate by the end of August.

WARSAW

In the pre-dawn hours of 1 August the spearheads of the 2nd Tank Army reached Praga, a suburb of Warsaw located on the eastern bank of the Vistula. An unpleasant surprise awaited the Soviets as they arrived at the outskirts – it turned out that Praga had been heavily fortified and de facto had been transformed into a modern fortress. All of a sudden, Radzievsky's entire tank army got stranded and was unable to maneuver: the way to the west was barred by the river, to the northwest – by the Praga fortifications, while to the north, northeast and east – by the panzers of 9. Army. But the worst was yet to come – on the same day General von Vormann launched sharp counterattacks simultaneously from several directions: "Hermann Goering" Panzer-Division and 19. Panzer-Division from the west/northwest, 4. Panzer Division from the north, and *"Wiking"* and *"Totenkopf"* from the east.

Sd.Kfz. 251/9 Ausf. D Kannonwagen armored half-tracks of III. Battalion/SS-Panzer-Grenadier-Regiment 9 "Germania" of 5. SS-Panzer-Division "Wiking" in action in Eastern Poland, the summer of 1944. (Detlev Terlisten)

Sd.Kfz. 251/9 Ausf. D Kannonwagen armored half-tracks of III. Battalion/SS-Panzer-Grenadier-Regiment 9 "Germania" of 5. SS-Panzer-Division "Wiking" in action in Eastern Poland, the summer of 1944. (Detlev Terlisten)

Sd.Kfz. 251/9 Ausf. D Kannonwagen armored half-tracks of III. Battalion/SS-Panzer-Grenadier-Regiment 9 "Germania" of 5. SS-Panzer-Division "Wiking" in action in Eastern Poland, the summer of 1944. (Detlev Terlisten)

Sd.Kfz. 251/9 Ausf. D Kannonwagen armored half-tracks of III. Battalion/SS-Panzer-Grenadier-Regiment 9 "Germania" of 5. SS-Panzer-Division "Wiking" in action in Eastern Poland, the summer of 1944. (Detlev Terlisten)

An especially critical situation emerged in the zone of Radzievsky's leading formation, the 3rd Tank Corps. It was completely surrounded and spent three days in desperate all-around defense before its remnants were finally able to breakout. It came out of the cauldron totally decimated – by 6 August the corps had lost 98 tanks and self-propelled guns, 20 artillery pieces, and 1,265 men in killed, wounded and missing. The overall damage inflicted on the 2nd Army was also heavy – from 1 to 10 August it had lost 284 tanks and self-propelled guns, and more than 2,300 men.

Leutnant Reinhard Peters, Acting Company Commander with Panzer-Regiment 35 (4. Panzer-Division) recalls how the spearhead of the 2nd Tank Army, the 3rd Tank Corps, was stopped at Warsaw:

> Beginning of August—A large Russian armored formation was advancing on Warsaw. It was supposed to be stopped. Panzer-Regiment 35 received the mission to take Radzymin from the east. The Panther battalion was directed to be the spearhead, but it was still refueling and rearming. As was so often the case, the 2nd Battalion moved out first.
>
> It was early in the afternoon when the city appeared, palpably close, in front of us. The only approach road from the east led through marshy terrain across a high embankment. We went into attack positions along a hedgerow that ran perpendicular to the road. Generalfeldmarschall Model had assembled a group of generals next to my Panzer IV. He aired his displeasure concerning the delay on the troop movements to the generals. When it was time for our former division commander, General von Saucken, to receive his due, he simply dropped his monocle and said with a quiet voice: "You'll not do that to me, Herr Feldmarschall." Then he turned away. We furtively grinned.
>
> What was about to transpire was anything but a textbook tank attack. We had to move across that damned embankment in single file. It was a dream for the Russian antitank guns and tanks, which were said to have run out of fuel. We were skeptical in that regard. I sent Leutnant Graf Moltke out with his platoon of tanks. We remained in ambush positions with the remaining tanks to provide covering fire, if needed. The platoon reached the edge of the city without encountering the enemy. We followed. At the marketplace, I had pairs of tanks move out along each of the streets that emanated like a star from there. We were all by ourselves next to a church. Suddenly, we heard tank tracks behind us. A T-34 was approaching us. He had turned his turret to the rear. My gunner initially took up a sight picture of a tank that had already been knocked out at the edge of the market place. More to the right," I yelled at him. Finally, he had the tank in his optics. The antitank round raced out of the barrel and brought the colossus 10 meters from us to a standstill. It was high time, since he would have rammed us a few seconds later. [22]

AFV STRENGTH OF THE PANZER-DIVISIONS OF 9. ARMY,
1 August 1944

4. Panzer-Division: 5 Pz III (3 operational), 83 Pz IV (45), 58 Pz V (40)
19. Panzer-Division: N/A
Panzer-Division "Hermann Goering": 62 Pz IV (50), 8 FlakPz 38 (7)
3. SS-Panzer-Division *"Totenkopf"*: 1 Pz III (1), 25 Pz IV (19), 57 Pz V (21), 8 Pz VI (1), 48 StuG (10)
5. SS-Panzer-Division *"Wiking"*: 24 Pz IV (12), 66 Pz V (42), 20 StuG (11)

The account of Martin Steiger, the company commander of 1./SS-Panzer-Regiment 3, summarizes best the struggle of the *"Totenkopf"* Division against the 8th Guards Tank Corps:

> The "Wiking" and "Totenkopf" Divisions were assigned to the newly established general command IV., SS-Panzerkorps Gille, on 10 August.
>
> The Korps was put into defensive action east of Warsaw. Enemy artillery fire hammered for days as, attack after attack, the Russians rolled against our already very weak lines. The superiority of the enemy was immense.
>
> The gaps along the front grew larger, often a grenadier only every 100 to 200 meters.
>
> Once again, we played the firefighters of the east.
>
> We lived from one attack to the next, from one shortening of the front to the next. Withdrawals of a few kilometers were followed by counterattacks to relieve neighboring units.
>
> We stood 30 kilometers east of Warsaw and held off the Russian masses with only a few Panzers left.

22 Schäufler, "Knight's Cross Panzers".

Enemy tanks, growing in numbers like flies, broke through, destroyed supply units, and kept fighting well behind our lines. We were thrown at them, knocked them out, and lost some more of our Panzers in the process. When we returned again to where our main front line had been only the day before when we left it, we found it captured already by the Russians. This happened almost every day. The losses of men and Panzers were staggering.

A new order awaited us at the Abteilung command post. [23]

* * *

A Soviet officer stares at a knocked-out Sd.Kfz. 251/1 Ausf. D armored half-track of III. Battalion/SS-Panzer-Grenadier-Regiment 6 "Theodor Eicke" of 3. SS-Panzer-Division "Totenkopf" somewhere in the vicinity of Warsaw 1944. (Roman Timokhin)

In the meantime the situation of the German 9. Army became very complicated, because on 1 August, when the 2nd Tank Army was about to enter Praga, *Armia Krajowa* launched an uprising in Warsaw. The non-communist Polish resistance was anxious because the USSR had already assumed direct control over the eastern part of Poland and had initiated the formation of the Lublin Committee to control the Soviet-occupied Polish territory. Hoping to gain control of the Polish capital before the 1st Byelorussian Front could "liberate" it, the freedom fighters of *Armia Krajowa* spontaneously decided to revolt.

The Red Army could benefit in many ways from the uprising. But Stalin decided that the Soviet Union must distance itself from the event and to pretend that it simply didn't exist. One day before the outbreak of the insurrection he even ordered all units of the *Armia Krajowa* to be disarmed and their officers – arrested. The complete ignorance of the Warsaw Uprising caused a serious concern among the Western Allies. London and Washington put pressure through diplomatic channels and on 21 August the Kremlin dictator agreed to help. But it was going to be a half-hearted attempt at best.

* * *

Following the debacle of the 2nd Tank Army in the flatlands to the east of Warsaw, the 2nd Tank Army was temporarily disbanded. The army's staff and the badly mauled 3rd Tank Corps were pulled off the frontline to rest and refit. The other two formations were employed in a quite smart manner – the 16th Tank Corps sent to reinforce the critically important Magnuszew bridgehead, while the 8th Guards Tank Corps was to support the offensive of the friendly forces to the east/northeast of the capital.

The catastrophe east of Praga didn't discourage Stalin. He instructed Rokossovsky to keep implementing the original plan and to try to outflank the city to the north. The focal point shifted to the sector of the 70th Army, which returned to the battlefield

23 Fey, op.cit, p. 114.

One of the main reasons for the failure of the 47th and 70th Armies to achieve a clean breakthrough was that their opponents practiced active defense, counterattacking at every opportunity. Eric Lehmkuhl of the Tiger company of *"Totenkopf"* recalls one such counterattack that took place on 20 August northeast of Praga:

> The Tiger of SS-Oberscharführer Weitner is knocked out. All his crew are killed. The Tiger of SS-Untersturmführer Neff is hit, sustains severe damage, and the crew bail out. The company carries out several counterattacks in the area of Radzymin and Pustelnik; we suffer some Tiger losses. Loader Boxleitner is killed by friendly fire. The Russians constantly attack us with artillery fire. Sleep is hard to come by, and life is to a degree unbearable. Currently, our armor is located in the area of Radzymin. SS-Obersturmbannführer Neidhardt is surveying the terrain with binoculars when a grenade explodes nearby, wounding him and killing his dog. The company is taken over by Neff. SS-Untersturmführer Kriescher is slightly wounded, and SS-Sturmmann Berg is wounded.

Marshals Rokossovsky and Zhukov discuss the military situation in the sector of the 65th Army. The photo was taken in October 1944 during the heavy battles for the Serock bridgehead on the western bank of the Narew. (Author's collection). (RinP)

> The front line has to be pulled back to the area of Jozefow. There are some dominant heights in the area. In the late afternoon, we receive orders to support the StuG battalion and take Hill 104 near Rembelszczyzna. The Russians have occupied the hill; we quickly advance up it and knock out a T-34 that is blocking our way at a range of fifty meters. In the morning the Russians open fire on us with artillery from the direction of Solchew. I've never seen anything like this. Thank God for a small ravine in which we take cover. Fountains of earth and trees are thrown through the air. To our front there is a loud bang, and we see a StuG get thrown into the air.
>
> The Tiger is shaken for about thirty minutes. The Russians laid artillery fire that fell behind us before masses of Russian infantry came toward us. Our own infantry are happy as we open fire with our 8.8cm and MG. This brings the Russians to a standstill. There is hardly any cover for them, but the pressure is so intense from the Russians that we have to fall back from the hill. Soon our own artillery and Nebelwerfer units shell the Russians, and then we roll forward back up the hill and try to reach a ravine which leads into a wood. The wood is just a sea of tree stumps and rubble, shot-up guns, and destroyed vehicles—amongst all this carnage are dead bodies from both sides.
>
> The hill is once again back in our hands. On the left is another Tiger, and on our right are two StuG's. There is a silence, and then we begin to hear the moaning of the wounded. There is a frenzied banging on my hatch. SS-Untersturmführer Neff and his gunner had bailed out after his Tiger was hit. Loader Mauser, driver Lucht, and radio operator Laux have all been killed. Eventually, things begin to settle down. The Russians don't press us, but on another morning, the third battle begins. There is no cover, no trees—we have to move back with the turret at the six o'clock position. We have a probation infantry battalion (a penal unit) assigned to us. We are ordered to attack back up the hill under the heaviest fire; in fact, the Russians are so demoralized that they don't even return fire, so we are back on top of the hill. The probation infantry battalion did nothing of note and hid from the Russians. Suddenly, it's midnight.
>
> Then came a radio signal to pull back, so we move to the foot of the hill where there is a wood. Here we find time to catch up on some needed sleep. We sleep inside the Tiger. I awake at about noon due to one of my friends snoring loudly, but standing before us is a group of Russians who are shouting at us and at the same time admiring our Tiger. I shout at my fellow comrades to wake up. Very quickly, we fire our MG at them, but we get hit from the right by antitank fire,

During the bloody fighting for the so-called "wet triangle" north of Warsaw in October 1944 both sides sustained heavy losses. This Pz IV Ausf. J tank of 2. Company/SS-Panzer-Regiment 5 of 5. SS-Panzer-Division "Wiking" was knocked out by one of the units of the 4th Artillery Corps of the 1st Byelorussian Front. (TsAMO)

> but nothing happens. We are asking ourselves where the gun is. We fire at the closest proximity with our main gun and drive at full gas down the road and reach our nearest infantry, which is still positioned on Hill 104. This was one of the closest experiences I had during the war. [24]

The situation in the sector defended by *"Wiking"* was no different. *Obersturmführer* Senghas, the commander of Headquarters Company of SS-Panzer-Regiment 5 wrote the following about an encounter with one of the units of 8th Guards Tank Corps that took place on 19 August:

> The night that followed also passed quietly. The next morning, however, the Russians laid down barrage fire with artillery and mortars for half an hour on our positions but concentrating on the friendly forces to the left. Towards 1000 hours, four enemy tanks moved north and quickly disappeared in the vegetated terrain.
> An hour later, the enemy attacked our positions once more form the woods. Since my men did not have any machine guns, I had the radio operator machine guns taken off the tanks and had them emplaced in our positions to good effect. When the Russian infantry had closed to about 600 meters, three of the four tanks suddenly appeared that we had seen previously, apparently wanting to support the Russian attack. One of my Panzer IV's knocked out all three in a short span of time; the fourth one was eliminated by the infantry on the left wing. The enemy tanks — T-34's and Shermans — immediately caught fire and blew apart a short while later. The Russian attack then bogged down forward of our positions. When the enemy attacked again two hours later, a heavy antitank gun was destroyed.
> Towards 1600 hours, a report was received from the right that the Russians had broken through in the sector of the "Westland" Regiment. I was then able to explain why we had been continuously receiving fire from the rear for more than an hour. When we ran out of ammunition at 1900 hours—the tanks had long since shot off their ammunition — and the front lines in the sector of the friendly forces to the left were being pulled back, we pulled back by circuitous routes. The village of Zazdros, which was right behind us, had been occupied by the enemy for some time. [25]

By the end of August the combined efforts of the 47th, 70th and 65th Armies finally produced some results. The Germans were squeezed into a small bridgehead northeast and east of Warsaw. The critical situation forced *Generaloberst* Georg-Hans Reinhardt, the new commander of Army Group "Center", immediately to transfer there 19. Panzer-Division to reinforce the important foothold. In the meantime, the 65th Army of General Batov succeeded in crossing the Narew and establishing a small bridgehead on its western bank near Serock. This led to further dispersion of the German forces because *"Wiking"*, reinforced with elements of 19. Panzer-Division, was expeditiously redeployed to the endangered sector.

24 Wood, op.cit.

25 Klapdor, op.cit, pp. 345-346.

The Germans were well aware that every bridgehead was a ticking bomb that could explode when it was least expected. In particular, the loss of the east bank of the Narew north of Serock increased the possibility of a northern envelopment of the Axis positions in the entire Warsaw area. That's why the defenders did everything possible to eliminate the dangerous foothold without delay. During the first days of September *"Wiking"*, additionally strengthened with some infantry and panzers, launched a series of fierce counterattacks against the positions of the 65th Army at Serock. The men of General Batov, however, withstood the assaults.

Many of the German attacks against the bridgehead failed, because the troops ordered to support *"Wiking"* were not of good quality. This finds confirmation in the after-action report of SS-Panzer-Regiment 5 of 10 September 1944. It describes a failed attack of two companies (one with Pz IVs and one equipped with Panthers), which objective had been the bridge over the Narew at Karniewec:

> As ordered, the company moved out at 0430 hours with four assault guns and one Panzer IV; it reached a general line 500 meters north of the cemetery to the left of the road.
> The friendly infantry, which only followed the guns hesitantly, lacked an aggressive spirit, and after casualties were taken after the first few hundred meters, it no longer advanced.
> I engaged heavy machine-gun nests and antitank rifles with the guns. The Panzer IV received an antitank gun hit in the right drive sprocket and, after an unsuccessful attempt to retrieve it, received another hit in the fighting compartment, which resulted in a total loss of the Panzer IV.
> While the company attempted to rally the friendly infantry forward once more by holding on to the line described above, two tank commanders and four men of the company were wounded. I personally was slightly wounded and pulled back to the line of departure at 0520 hours as the last assault gun. […]
> The attack, which was conducted after a preceding friendly artillery preparation of only 20 to 30 shells against well-constructed field fortifications of the enemy, could not be crowned with success due to the numerical inferiority (Force ratio: 1:20). I had the impression that the attacks on the bridgehead were not properly prepared from on high. In any event, there was no cohesiveness in the command and control to any great degree. [26]

26 Ibid., pp. 361-362.

* * *

With all German troops finally pushed to the Vistula and the Narew, Rokossovsky decided that the time had come to eliminate the Praga stronghold, which had become a thorn in the flesh of the 1st Byelorussian Front. As it was previously mentioned, the place had been heavily fortified and *de facto* had become a fortress. This required additional forces to be brought in the sector of the 47th Army and because of that Rokossovsky in the first days of September relocated the 1st Polish Army and the 8th Guards Tank Corps to the Warsaw area.

The onslaught began on 10 September. The defenders (73. Infantry Division and elements of *"Totenkopf"*) were hit hard. To blast the defenders out of their strongpoints and bunkers, the Soviets and Poles used not only explosive charges, but also tanks, direct-laying guns (including super-heavy 203-mm howitzers), 'Boston' level-bombers and Il-2 Shturmoviks. In a desperate attempt to save Praga from falling, *General der Panzertruppe* Smilo von Lüttwitz, the new commander of 9. Army, moved there 19. Panzer-Division. But it was too little, too late. By 14 September the Soviet and Polish assault groups completely cleared the place. The badly beaten German garrison retreated to the north.

On 16 September, on orders from Moscow, Rokossovsky made his sole effort to establish contact with the insurgents still fighting in his birth city. It could be described as half-hearted at best. Elements of two Polish divisions forced the river and established small bridgeheads on the western bank, securing several blocks in the process. Save for some mortars and 45-mm anti-tank guns, the assault battalions had no other heavy weapons at their disposal. They were supported from the eastern bank by Polish artillery, but not by the Soviet artillery and air force. As in many other cases, the Germans reacted immediately and launched resolute counterattacks against the unfortunate and inexperienced Poles. (Elements of several panzer divisions had been moved into Warsaw to suppress the uprising.) Within a week the Polish battalions were decimated and on 16 September the survivors were evacuated back to the eastern bank.

By the end of September the brave Polish insurgents were already critically short of everything and it was apparent that the uprising was coming to its logical end. On 2 October Warsaw surrendered. But the battle in the area was far from over.

On 4 October 1944 Weiss' 2. Army attacked the Serock bridgehead with strong forces (including 3. and 25. Panzer-Divisions and two full-strength battalions of Tiger tanks). The men of General Batov, however, offered spirited resistance and withstood the onslaught.

Two more Pz IV Ausf. J tanks of 2. Company/SS-Panzer-Regiment 5 of 5. SS-Panzer-Division "Wiking" lost during the heavy fighting for the "wet triangle". They were knocked out by the 152-mm howitzers of the 86th Heavy Howitzer Artillery Brigade at the village of Michałów-Reginów. (TsAMO)

The official history of 3. Panzer-Division gives a vivid description of the German offensive:

> The night of 3–4 October slowly came to an end. At that point, the sound of hundreds of German artillery pieces could be heard barking. The soldiers in the trenches jumped up with a fright. They hadn't experienced anything like that in years. There was a howling and screeching headed over towards the enemy's side. The unmistakable sound of rockets from the Nebelwerfer could be heard above the rest as they churned up the ground. A short while later, the divisions moved out.
>
> Once again, the 3. Panzer-Division was the wing division. It was clear from the outset that the flanks would become longer and more exposed as the attack proceeded. The terrain consisted of hillocks that were covered in vegetation and deep woods. Two Tiger battalions were attached to the division, and they formed the spearhead. Hauptmann Voigts's II./Panzer-Regiment 6 followed in the second wave. The Russians were so shaken up by the preparatory fires that they proved incapable of offering any serious resistance. The fighting vehicles moved right through the enemy's front lines and soon found themselves among his artillery before the enemy started to regain his composure. The resistance grew more stubborn by the hour. The mechanized infantry lost contact with the tanks, since they were attacked several times in the flanks.
>
> The farther the tanks advanced, the tougher the Russian resistance became. The enemy riflemen had established themselves in well-constructed field fortifications that were terrifically camouflaged. By early afternoon, the Tigers stalled in front of the enemy's antitank-gun fire. The 5th, 6th, and 8th Companies of the armored regiment were then called forward. Two assault guns from the 5th Company were lost during the approach through mines. But *Oberleutnant* Aschermann was soon there with his vehicles and extended the front the Tigers had created to the right. The assault guns maneuvered to find good firing positions from which to engage the Russian antitank guns. The assault guns of *Feldwebel* Beckenfelder and Inter were hit. By then, the 6th Company of *Oberleutnant* Weh and the 8th Company of *Oberleutnant* Lope had also arrived. Both of the companies enveloped from the right, hit the Soviets in the flank and overran approximately twenty enemy antitank guns. The 8th Company lost three tanks and had to pull back. *Oberleutnant* Lope's tank was knocked out. He was captured but was able to escape two hours later and make his way back to German lines.
>
> The two Tiger battalions then attempted the third run at the enemy positions. They wanted to exploit the path that had been created by the division's armored vehicles and cover the last few kilometers to the Narew. It had become late afternoon by then and time was pressing, if the Germans wanted to eject the enemy before the onset of darkness. The Tigers advanced in a death-defying manner into the enemy positions, but the Russian resistance only seemed to intensify. Artillery

A German position silenced by one of the units of the 4th Artillery Corps during the heavy fighting for the "wet triangle" in October 1944. These rocket launchers (30 cm Nebelwerfer 42) fell intact in Soviet hands. (TsAMO)

A heavily fortified German position at the "wet triangle" softened-up by the guns and mortars of the 4th Artillery Corps, and overran by the Soviet infantry. On the photo one can see an MG 42 machinegun, an empty ammunition box and two Model 1924 Stielhandgranate hand grenades. (TsAMO)

> shells were also coming in from the far bank of the Narew for the continuation of the land and landing among the steel animals. The men of the armor regiment were amazed as to how much punishment a Tiger could take and then continue to move. But, in the end, the effort was futile. And it was only two kilometers to the Narew. It could not be done. The Russians did not waver, and they used their advantage in artillery. [27]

By 10 October the German attacks had already shot their bolt. Shortly afterwards the 65th Army launched an offensive of its own and even succeeded in expanding the Serock bridgehead further to the west.

In the meantime Rokossovsky had undertaken yet another major assault against a bitterly defended German bastion. On 10 October the forces of three armies (47th, 70th and 1st Polish) attacked the positions of IV-SS Panzer Corps in the so-called "wet triangle" immediately to the north of Warsaw. The men of the two crack SS-Panzer Divisions, *"Wiking"* and *"Totenkopf"*, however, withstood the onslaught. Attack after attack was beaten back with heavy losses on the Soviets and Poles, and on 28 October the operation was canceled for good.

Eric Lehmkuhl of the Tiger company of *"Totenkopf"* gives a brief recollection of the battle in the "wet triangle":

> October comes—we have built bunkers in the area of Jozefow. During an artillery raid, I fall over and break my arm. I'm taken to a field hospital in Modlin. On 9 October, I return to the company to recover. Since the tenth, the Russians had started another offensive with 1,000 guns along a five-kilometer front in our divisional sector. Like an earthquake, the barrage reaches Jozefow, and the Russians break through several sectors of our front line, but later in the day, our former front-line positions are restored. On the twelfth, I returned to the company commander's Tiger and the crew of SS-Untersturmführer Neff. We see action in the area of Legionowo - Jablonna in the so-called wet triangle near the Vistula River. SS-Unterscharführer Probst and SS-Rottenführer Hodap are both killed near Jablonna. One of our cooks is killed on a farm near Jablonna by a mortar round.[28]

---

27 "Armored Bears", Vol. 2, Mechanicsburg, Stackpole Books, 2013.

28 Wood, op. cit..

Another German position silenced by the 4th Artillery Corps during the heavy fighting for the "wet triangle" in October 1944. TsAMO)

The after-action report of the 2. Company of SS-Panzer-Regiment 5 on the fighting of 13 October is far more detailed:

> The enemy had succeeded in breaking through west of the security line of the company during the morning hours and establishing himself just short of the Wieliszew — Nieporent rail line. By doing so, the enemy succeeded in cutting off the company and elements of the infantry with his strong forces.
> At 1100 hours, orders arrived from the battalion commander to pull back with the remaining infantry forces and occupy new positions behind the railway embankment in the sector of the reconnaissance battalion. The enemy positions were overrun in a short engagement and a new security line was established. As a result of additional attacks by the enemy to the right of us, he succeeded in breaking through all the way to the rail station in Wieleszew and, as a result, cutting off the retreat route for the battalion, the remaining elements of the infantry and the reconnaissance battalion. As the result of the sudden appearance of several enemy tanks, a great deal of hubbub arose among the infantry, which immediately pulled back to the location of our tanks. As the result of heavy enemy artillery fire, one tank was set alight by a direct hit; in addition, one vehicle with front differential problems was set alight by our own vehicles, because there were no recovery means available.
> Since the enemy pressure continued to increase, the battalion, together with the remnants of the infantry and the reconnaissance battalion, had to pull back to Wieliszew. After reaching our own positions, the company was committed to an immediate counterattack against the patch of woods south of Nieporent to restore the old main line of resistance along the railway embankment. After completing the mission, the company pulled back as far as the edge of the woods and screened to the east. Destroyed were 2 4.7-centimeter antitank guns, 2 trucks, 10 machine guns; enemy losses: 30-40 men.[29]

29 Klepdor, op.cit, pp. 373-374.

CHAPTER 7

THE OFFENSIVES IN EAST PRUSSIA AND POMERANIA

NEW ASSIGNMENT

On the evening of 12 November 1944 Stalin called Rokossovsky and informed him that he had been appointed commander of the 2nd Byelorussian Front. It is difficult to say why the dictator had decided to replace him with Zhukov, but perhaps this had something to do with the series of defeats sustained by the 1st Byelorussian Front at the gates of Warsaw. It is quite probable that Stalin was concerned that the same might happen at the gates of Berlin (once the Front would get there). He also managed to calm the Marshal, assuring him that the 2nd Byelorussian Front was no longer going to be a second-rate formation, but would be massively reinforced, because its forces were going to play a very important role in the forthcoming winter offensive.

Stalin indeed kept his promise and the 2nd Byelorussian Front beefed up in no time. In a matter of month or so, the Front grew from four to seven armies, and also got a tank army. Moreover, the 4th Air Army was also strengthened and nearly doubled its size. All this was done on purpose: the 2nd Byelorussian Front was to deliver a smashing attack in the direction of the Gulf of Danzig, thereby trapping the main body of the German Army Group "Center" in East Prussia.

Rokossovsky was familiar with the new assignment of the Front – after all, in August he had planned an attack with the right wing of the 1st Byelorussian Front towards Thorn. He also knew quite well about half of the armies that now were under him, because he had led them during various stages of Operation "Bagration".

The offensive was to be executed in typical Soviet manner. An extremely powerful "shock" group was to be formed on the Front's left flank comprising four armies, a tank army, three armored corps and a cavalry corps. They were to attack from two large bridgeheads on the western bank of the Narew.

In the Serock bridgehead, on the Front's extreme left wing, were positioned the 70th and 65th Armies. The latter was reinforced with the full-strength 1st Guards Tank Corps. It was definitely a very unusual armored formation, because it was equipped with JS-2 heavy tanks and SU-100 tank destroyers instead of the "regular" T-34/85.

Further north, in the Różan bridgehead, the most powerful of all Rokossovsky's task forces was deployed. It was made up of 2nd Shock and 48th Armies, which were reinforced with an armored corps each. (8th Guards Tank Corps and 8th Mechanized Corps, respectively.) Behind them was placed the second wave, the 5th Guards Tank Army and the 3rd Guards Cavalry Corps. They were to act as exploitation forces that were to break into open country once the German defense was penetrated. The right flank of that "shock" was protected by 49th Army, further to the north was positioned the 3rd Army; the Front's extreme right wing was entrusted to the 50th Army.

The troops of the Front spent the two months preceding the offensive in extensive training. The emphasis was on the breaching of fortified positions, as well as on pursuit of retreating enemy remnants. Special attention was paid on establishing of the so-called forward detachments, relatively small highly mobile groups, which were meant to become the main instrument of the pursuit. Enormous quantities of ammunition, fuel and food were stockpiled. It can safely be said that when the East Prussian Operation was finally unleashed in mid-January 1945, the 2nd Byelorussian Front was fully prepared, supplied and in excellent condition.

* * *

Rokossovsky was also quite familiar with the enemy formation opposing him – it was the German 2. Army that was still led by his old nemesis *Generaloberst* Walter Weiss. It consisted of ten infantry divisions occupying the main line of resistance and the 7. Panzer-Division held in reserve at Zichenau (Ciechanów). There were also several powerful assets, namely the Heavy-Panzer-Battalion 507 (King Tigers) and six assault-gun brigades, all of them fully equipped.

Apparently, the quiet period had allowed the Germans to strengthen, reinforce and resupply the divisions holding the main line of resistance, because by the beginning of the Soviet offensive they were in pretty good overall condition. They were occupying solid, heavily fortified positions, but there was nothing behind them – save for 7. Panzer-Division Weiss had no significant reserves whatsoever.

THE EAST PRUSSIAN OPERATION

The offensive of the 2nd Byelorussian Front kicked off on the morning of 14 January 1945, following a tremendous artillery barrage. The Soviet assault battalions managed to overcome the fanatical German defense and by midday in many places they were already clearing the third trench line. General Weiss reacted immediately and ordered all corps' and divisional reserves to be committed right away. But they were way too weak to check the Soviet avalanche.

On the next day both Weiss and Rokossovsky committed reserves to battle. The former threw into action 7. Panzer-Division, while the latter released 1st Guards Tank Corps and 8th Guards Tank Corps. Moreover, on 16 January the M4 Sherman-equipped 8th Mechanized Corps was pushed through the gap in the German defense and on 17 January the formidable 5th Guards Tank Army was finally brought into play. Weiss' attempt to stop them by counterattacking with Panzer-Grenadier *"Grossdeutschland"* produced no results and before long the entire front of 2. Army disintegrated. Then the hard pressed German divisions began a disorganized retreat to the northwest, abandoning their heavy weapons and equipment.

A column of Soviet T-34/85 tanks (painted in winter camouflage) of one of the armored corps of the 2nd Byelorussian Front is about to enter the battle. Poland/East Prussia, the second half of January 1945. (RinP)

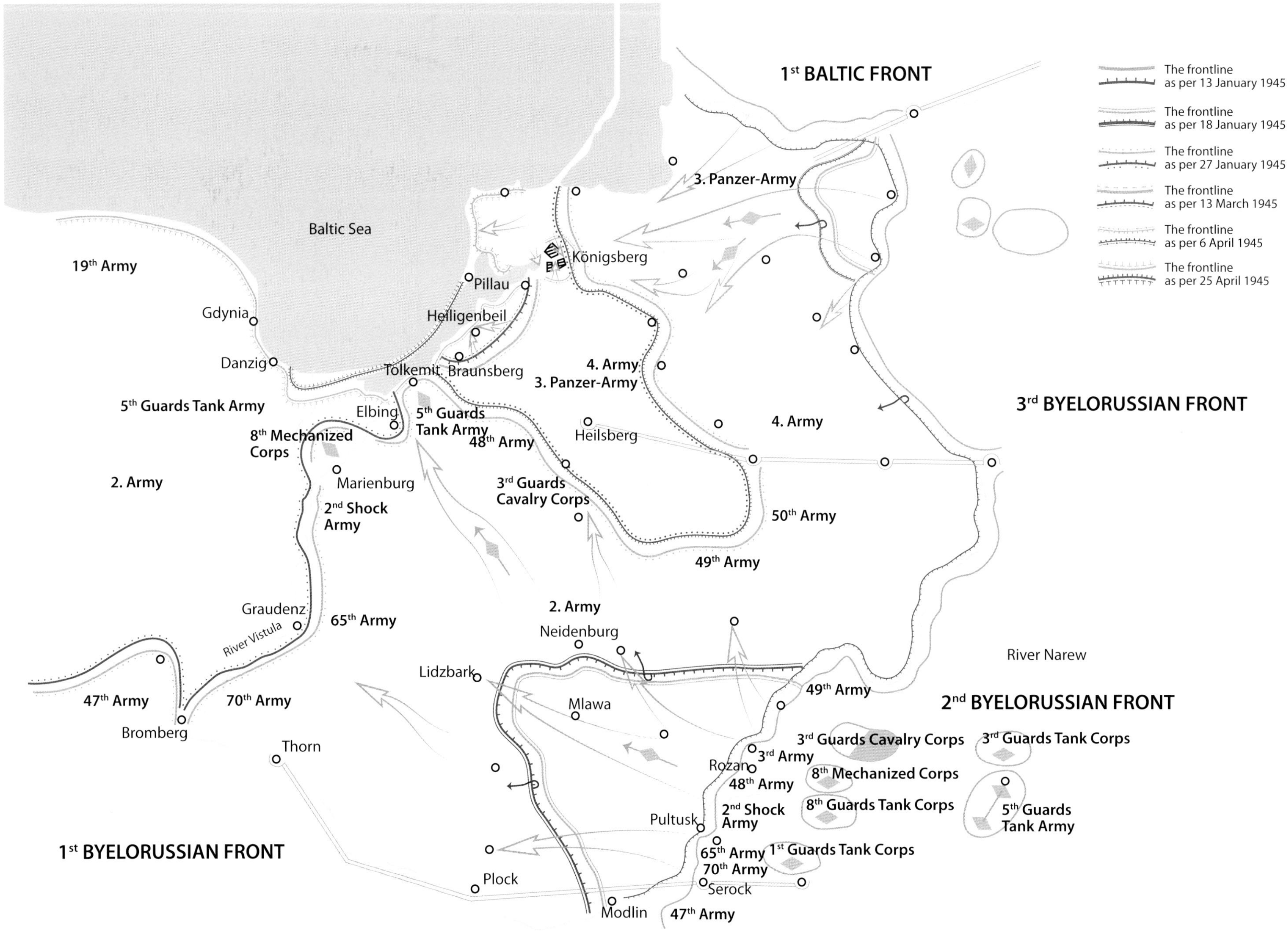

1st BALTIC FRONT
The frontline as per 13 January 1945
The frontline as per 18 January 1945
The frontline as per 27 January 1945
The frontline as per 13 March 1945
The frontline as per 6 April 1945
The frontline as per 25 April 1945
3. Panzer-Army
Baltic Sea
Königsberg
19th Army
Pillau
Gdynia
Heiligenbeil
Danzig
4. Army
Tolkemit
Braunsberg
3. Panzer-Army
5th Guards Tank Army
3rd BYELORUSSIAN FRONT
Elbing
5th Guards Tank Army
4. Army
8th Mechanized Corps
48th Army
Heilsberg
2. Army
Marienburg
3rd Guards Cavalry Corps
2nd Shock Army
50th Army
49th Army
2. Army
Graudenz
65th Army
Neidenburg
River Vistula
River Narew
Lidzbark
47th Army
70th Army
49th Army
Mlawa
2nd BYELORUSSIAN FRONT
Bromberg
3rd Guards Cavalry Corps
3rd Guards Tank Corps
Thorn
3rd Army
Rozan
8th Mechanized Corps
48th Army
8th Guards Tank Corps
2nd Shock Army
Pultusk
5th Guards Tank Army
1st BYELORUSSIAN FRONT
65th Army
1st Guards Tank Corps
70th Army
Plock
Serock
Modlin
47th Army

Soviet T-34/85 tanks, SU-100 self-propelled guns and infantry of the 5th Guards Tank Army break through the German field fortifications, Poland/East Prussia, the second half of January 1945. (RinP)

By 22 January the entire frontline of Army Group "Center' had been fragmented and de facto ceased to exist. On the same day the 5th Guards Tank Army reached the Baltic coast at Elbing. Shortly afterwards the Shermans of the 8th Mechanized Corps appeared at the gates of the Marienburg Fortress. Thus, the German forces that so resolutely and heroically defended East Prussia found themselves trapped in a cauldron.

The complete isolation of East Prussia caused a lot of trouble to the German High Command. On 27 January Hitler sacked Reinhardt and replaced him the Austrian-born *Generaloberst* Lothar Rendulic. The army group itself was officially re-designated Army Group "North".

On the same day encircled 4. Army launched a breakout to the west. The escapees were spearheaded by two armored formations – 24. Panzer-Division and Panzer-Grenadier *"Grossdeutschland"* – which due to various reasons were critically short of AFVs. The men of the Soviet 48th Army, which were standing in the path of the breakout force, miraculously succeeded in preventing the linkup. The situation of the trapped defenders of East Prussia deteriorated even further on 10 February, when the besieged town of Elbing fell in Soviet hands. From that moment the distance between the East Prussian cauldron and the "outer world" was so great that it was impossible to cover in a single attack.

THE POMERANIAN OPERATION

Around 10 February major changes occurred in the order of battle of the 2nd Byelorussian Front. Those armies that were engaged in action against the East Prussian cauldron (3rd, 48th and 5th Guards Tank Army) were handed over to the neighboring 3rd Byelorussian Front, while the rest were instructed to finish off the German forces in the eastern part of Pomerania (i.e. 2. Army). For that purpose Rokossovsky got two fresh formations from the Stavka reserves, the 19th Army and the 3rd Guards Tank Corps.

The offensive of 2nd Byelorussian Front resumed on 10 February. The main blow was delivered from a bridgehead west of Graudenz in a northwesterly direction. Right from the outset, however, the Soviets ran into very determined resistance and failed to break through. It turned out that in the meantime Weiss had reinforced the perimeter to south of Danzig with several divisions (including 4. Panzer-Division) freshly shipped from Courland and now was ready to fight for every meter of ground.

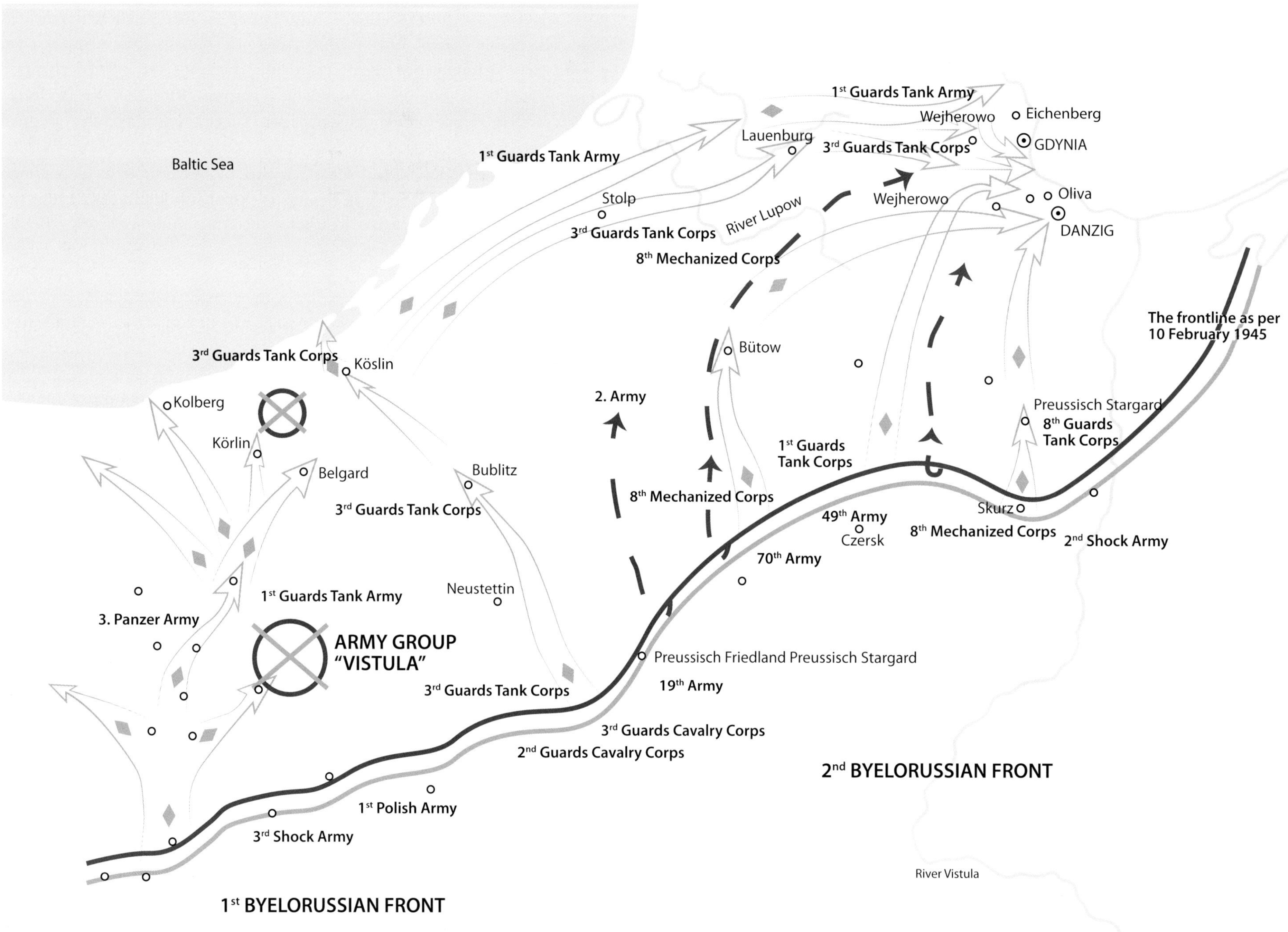
Baltic Sea
1st Guards Tank Army
Wejherowo
Eichenberg
Lauenburg
3rd Guards Tank Corps
GDYNIA
1st Guards Tank Army
Stolp
River Lupow
Wejherowo
Oliva
3rd Guards Tank Corps
DANZIG
8th Mechanized Corps
The frontline as per
10 February 1945
Bütow
3rd Guards Tank Corps
Köslin
Kolberg
2. Army
Preussisch Stargard
8th Guards
Tank Corps
Körlin
1st Guards
Tank Corps
Belgard
Bublitz
8th Mechanized Corps
3rd Guards Tank Corps
Skurz
49th Army
Czersk
8th Mechanized Corps
2nd Shock Army
70th Army
1st Guards Tank Army
Neustettin
3. Panzer Army
ARMY GROUP
"VISTULA"
Preussisch Friedland Preussisch Stargard
3rd Guards Tank Corps
19th Army
3rd Guards Cavalry Corps
2nd Guards Cavalry Corps
2nd BYELORUSSIAN FRONT
1st Polish Army
3rd Shock Army
River Vistula
1st BYELORUSSIAN FRONT

A German late Sd.Kfz. 7 prime mover with a 15 cm sFH 18 howitzer in tow destroyed on 16 January 1945 by the Il-2 Shturmoviks of the 4th Air Army at Królewo, northwest of Warsaw. (TsAMO)

Obergefreiter Peter Oberhuber, a tank driver with 6. Company/Panzer-Regiment 35 recalls the first action of 4. Panzer-Division in West Prussia:

> We were back on German soil since the end of January. We left our tanks in Kurland. From Gotenhafen, the crews were taken to the Graudenz Training Area on all sorts of vehicles. We were on a low boy. Completely unprotected, we were exposed to the biting cold and the sharp winds from the east. We received our new tanks there. The 2nd Battalion received Panzer IV's and a company of assault guns. The 1st Battalion had the Panther, with one company receiving the Jagdpanther. Those of us in the 2nd Battalion looked at the combat power of the 1st with a touch of envy. We then went back to Tuchel. The populace waved to us in a friendly manner.
>
> We had to go against Ivan in difficult defensive engagements day-in and day-out. Two times, three times a day, we conducted immediate counterattacks. Here, there, everywhere it seemed, in an effort to slow down the advance of the Red Army.
>
> 13 February 1945 — We marched through Tuchel to the south. A signpost told us we were outside of Liebenau. Tired and burned-out soldiers from a flight unit sat on the side of the road. They waved to us, since they knew that they certainly would have been captured by the Russians without us. We moved under a train overpass. We could already see the red tracer element of the Russian antitank rounds coming for us. A strong enemy armored formation was facing us. The 6th Company deployed by platoon and took up reverse-slope positions. Only the tank commanders were able to observe over the rise. The platoon leader directed that we were not to fire until he gave the order. The first three Russian tanks were nosing their way over the slope. A KV II [JS 2] was in the lead—unmistakable because of its massive turret. We opened fire like a thunderclap at 50 meters. Three Russians were soon on fire. The crews bailed out. The tanks that were following turned around quickly, but they received flanking fires from another platoon of the 6th. They fled as quickly as possible and disappeared into the village. We received orders to pursue and attack the village. A Tiger was attached to us, which had been with the regiment for some time. I do not know where the giant came from. All of a sudden it was with us, and it stayed with us.
>
> We first tried a frontal attack, but that did not work, because we received fire from every nook and cranny. So we went around the village and attacked from the side. The Tiger took a lot of work away from us, since it could crack open the Russian tanks at 2,000 meters with its 8.8-centimeter. We were not able to enter the village from that angle, either, since the enemy was quickly able to concentrate his weaponry against us. As a result, we swung farther out, so as to approach directly from the south. By then, it had become dark, however. The even plain proved deceptive. The ground underneath my tank collapsed all of a sudden. It had broken through the ice of a snow-covered creek. Water was running into the driver's hatch. We almost flipped over. It was only through luck and some cleverness that I was able to get out. But the Tiger — our pride and joy — was

A German Sd.Kfz. 252 armored ammunition carrier half-track destroyed on 16 January 1945 by the Il-2 Shturmoviks of the 4th Air Army at Królewo, northwest of Warsaw. The tactical symbol painted on the vehicle suggests that it had belonged to an assault-gun brigade. The prime mover and the howitzer from the previous photo are clearly visible in the background. (TsAMO)

> hopelessly drawn in due to its enormous weight. Our hearts ached when we received orders to move back to the line of departure and blow up the Tiger. [30]

Rokossovsky regrouped his forces and on 24 February yet another heavy blow fell on the German positions. In the first week of March his spearheads reached the Baltic coast. The result was a huge gap that emerged in the middle of the German front stretching from the mouth of the Oder to Danzig.

30 Schäufler, "Knight's Cross Panzers".

Determined to finish off the trapped enemy troops in West Prussia once and for all, Stalin placed the 1st Guards Tank Army of Colonel-General Katukov under the 2nd Byelorussian Front and ordered Rokossovsky to clear off the Gulf of Danzig as quickly as possible. (He needed additional forces for the upcoming final offensive on Berlin.) A month of very bloody fighting followed before West Prussia was completely secured. The remnants of 2. Army retreated to two "safe havens" that were impossible to take by direct attacks: the 35-km-long sand bar peninsula at the entrance of the gulf (known as the Hel Peninsula) and the very marshy mouth of the Vistula. They remained there till the end of the war.

This German late Pz IV Ausf. J tank, presumably of 7. Panzer-Division, was knocked-out on 17 January 1945 at Szumlin, northwest of Warsaw, by the Il-2 Shturmoviks of the 4th Air Army. (TsAMO)

An Sd.Kfz. 251/22 Ausf. D armored half-track and a Marder III Ausf. M tank-destroyer of 7. Panzer-Division knocked out on 16 January 1945 at Miszewo Wielkie, northwest of Warsaw, by the Il-2 Shturmoviks of the 4th Air Army. The former belonged to 8. Company/Panzer-Grenadier Regiment 6, the latter – most probably to 1. Company/Tank-Destroyer Battalion 42. (TsAMO)

West Prussia, February 1945. An Sd.Kfz. 251 Ausf. D armored half-track (most probably of 7. Company/Panzer-Grenadier Regiment 6, of 7. Panzer-Division), an Sd.Kfz. 7 prime mover and some trucks knocked by the Il-2 Shturmoviks of the 4th Air Army. Of interest is the 2cm KwK or Flak30 gun mounted on the Sd.Kfz. 251.(TsAMO)

A Soviet SU-76M self-propelled gun of undisclosed unit of the 2nd Byelorussian Front lost in combat. West Prussia, February 1945. A wood gas-generator has been installed in the truck in the left (on the second photo). (TsAMO)

West Prussia, February 1945. An Sd.Kfz. 234/2 Puma armored car of 1. Company/Panzer-Reconnaissance Battalion 7 of 7. Panzer-Division put out of action by the Il-2 Shturmoviks of the 4th Air Army. (TsAMO)

Soviet ISU-122 self-propelled guns of 8th Guards Tank Corps advance toward Danzig, March 1945. (TsAMO)

A German King Tiger tank of SS-Heavy-Panzer-Battalion 503 knocked out by one of the units of the 2nd Artillery Division in the vicinity of Danzig, late March 1945. It had been immobilized by a direct hit in the chassis. (TsAMO)

German military equipment lost in West Prussia in the spring of 1945 due to low-level attacks of the Il-2 Shturmoviks of the 4th Air Army: an 8.8 cm PaK 43 heavy anti-tank gun and a Jagdpanzer 38(t) Hetzer tank-destroyer. (TsAMO)

Weapons and vehicles of 7. Panzer-Division tossed in the Gulf of Danzig, early April 1945. On the photos one can see an Sd.Kfz. 251/22 armored half-track and a 15 cm sFH 18 howitzer. (RinP)

A Soviet JS-2 heavy tank of undisclosed unit of the 2nd Byelorussian Front with infantry riders enters Danzig, late March 1945. (TsAMO)

Soviet M4A2 Sherman tanks of the 8th Mechanized Corps with infantry mounted on them enter the ruined Danzig, late March 1945. (On the first photo one can see several ISU-122 heavy self-propelled guns accompanying the tank column.) (WA)

German field fortifications at Espenkrug (a suburb of Danzig) smashed by the Soviet 2nd Artillery Division, late March 1945. (TsAMO)

A German 8.8 cm Flak 36/37 heavy anti-aircraft gun abandoned at Oliva (a suburb of Danzig), late March 1945. The scene represents a makeshift firing position – the gun was hurriedly detached from the towing vehicle, an Sd.Kfz. 7 prime mover, and then abandoned in a hurry when the Soviets approached. (TsAMO)

A Soviet M4A2 Sherman tank of the 8th Mechanized Corps turned into a monument after the taking of Danzig, June 1945. Initially, it was placed in the city center; originally, there was an inscription 'Ivan Lagutin' on its turret. (NAC)

A German StuG III Ausf. G assault gun knocked out by one of the units of the 2nd Artillery Division at Zoppot, north of Danzig, late March 1945. (TsAMO) Note that this photo has been printed in reverse – the driver's visor is on the other side.

A German King Tiger tank of SS-Heavy-Panzer-Battalion 503 knocked out by one of the units of the 2nd Artillery Division at Oliva, a suburb of Danzig, late March 1945. (TsAMO)

German artillery pieces (a 8.8 cm Flak 36/37 heavy anti-aircraft gun and a 15 cm sFH 18 howitzer) abandoned in Oliva (a suburb of Danzig), late March 1945. (TsAMO)

CHAPTER 8

FROM THE ODER TO THE ELBE

PLANNING AND PREPARATIONS

The strategic goal of the Soviet Supreme Command in the Berlin Operation was to destroy the German forces defending the approaches to Berlin, seize the capital city of the Third Reich and link up with the Allied armies advancing from the west on the Elbe River. (By the beginning of April 1945 the American, British and Canadian armies were driving through Central Germany at full speed and their spearheads were mere 100-120 km from Berlin.) There were growing concerns within the Soviet military and political leadership that, despite the agreements, the Anglo-American armies would try to size the city. It was this concern, coupled with the perception that the German forces still engaged on the Western Front might turn eastwards, that accelerated the Soviet offensive preparations.

The formal General Staff's planning for Operation "Berlin" commenced on 1 April 1945, when Rokossovsky's Front was still mopping up the last German pockets of resistance at the Gulf of Danzig. On the very next day the Marshal flew to Moscow where he presented his operational concept. (Marshals Zhukov and Konev, the commanders of the 1st Byelorussian and 1st Ukrainian Fronts, were also present.) Following some lively discussions and thorough reviews of the plans brought by the three Front commanders, Stalin approved them and set the D-Day for 16 April. (The 2nd Byelorussian Front was to start its attack on 20 April in view of its redeployment from east to west.)

The plan developed by the Stavka called for several powerful blows delivered by the three Fronts. Berlin had to be encircled, while the enemy forces deployed in its vicinity had to be sliced into "pockets" and destroyed separately. Within 12-15 days the city had to be taken and contact with the advancing Allied armies had to be established along the Elbe.

The 2nd Byelorussian Front, which was yet to redeploy from the Danzig area, was to go over to the defensive two or three days after the other two Fronts. The "shock" group was to consist of three armies (65th, 70th and 49th), each of them with strong armor support (one armored corps). They were to attack across the Oder in the Stettin – Schwedt sector, annihilate the enemy forces in the vicinity of Stettin and prevent 3. Panzer-Army from reinforcing the German troops around Berlin. Subsequently, it was to advance to the west/northwest to occupy the northern part of the Brandenburg province and link up with the British 2nd Army along the lower Elbe.

* * *

Assembling the "shock" group was a major challenge for Rokossovsky and his staff, because it required an extensive regrouping over long distances during a critically short period. After all, by the beginning of April the main body of the 2nd Byelorussian Front was situated in Western Prussia, near Danzig, more than 500 km away from the Oder line. Five full-strength armies and a number of independent assets had to be redeployed to the west exactly when the railway network was overwhelmed with supplies needed for the forthcoming offensive. And all these repositions had to be completed within two weeks.

The redeployment was carried out by rail and by trucks. The traffic plan called

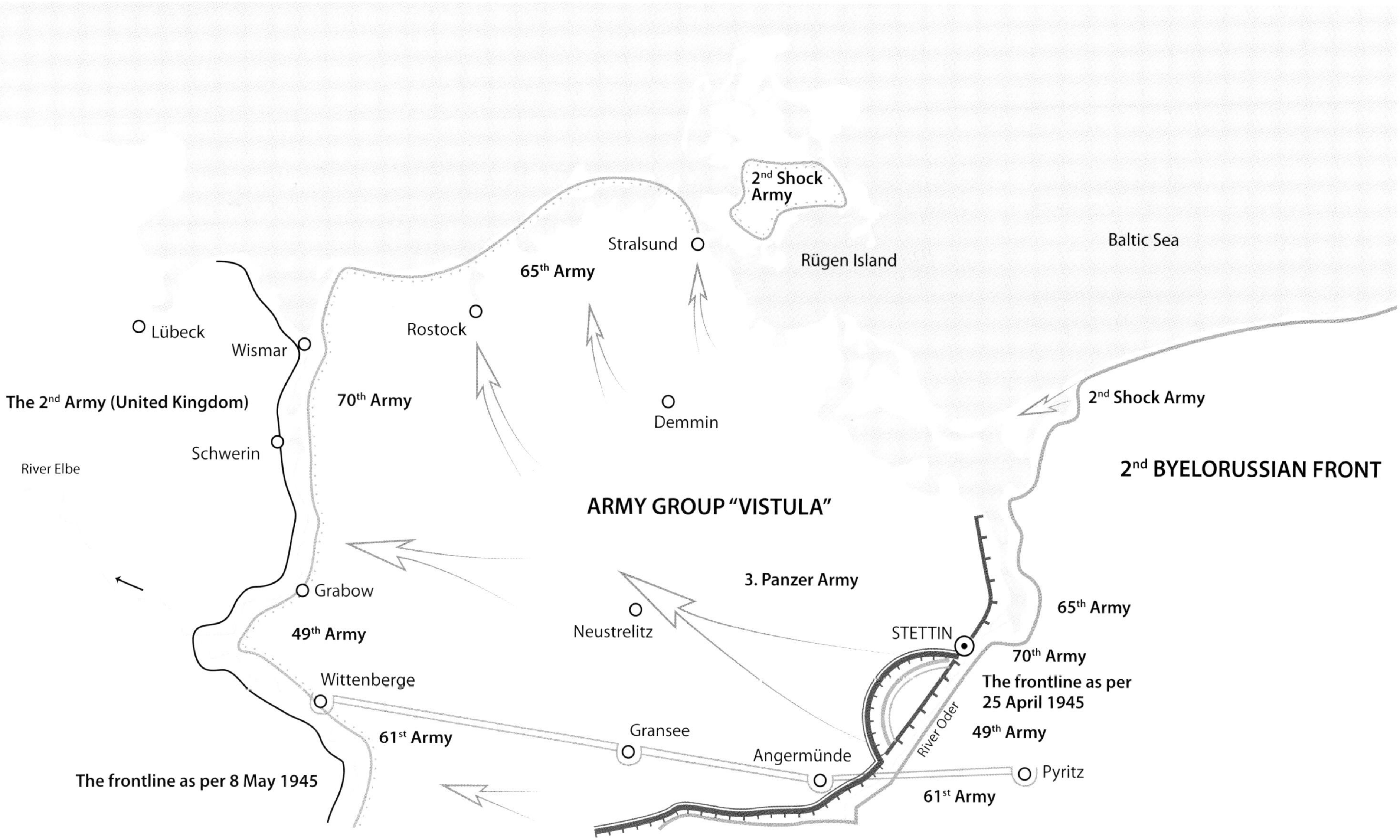
2nd Shock Army
Baltic Sea
Stralsund
Rügen Island
65th Army
Lübeck
Rostock
Wismar
70th Army
The 2nd Army (United Kingdom)
2nd Shock Army
Demmin
Schwerin
River Elbe
2nd BYELORUSSIAN FRONT
ARMY GROUP "VISTULA"
3. Panzer Army
Grabow
65th Army
Neustrelitz
49th Army
STETTIN
70th Army
Wittenberge
The frontline as per 25 April 1945
River Oder
Gransee
61st Army
49th Army
Angermünde
Pyritz
The frontline as per 8 May 1945
61st Army

An Opel Maultier half-track truck of a Waffen-SS unit destroyed by the Il-2 Shturmoviks of the 4th Air Army in the vicinity of Kunow, southwest of Stettin, late April 1945. (TsAMO)

A vehicle carrying German troops destroyed by the Il-2 Shturmoviks of the 4th Air Army in the vicinity of Casekow, southwest of Stettin, late April 1945. (TsAMO)

A German Panther Ausf. D tank destroyed on 20 April 1945 at Kolbitzow (a village just southwest of Stettin) by PTAB bombs dropped by Il-2 Shturmoviks of the 4th Air Army. The Panther most probably had belonged to Panzer-Training Formation "Ostsee". (TsAMO)

for a daily march of 40-45 km for a combined-service column. All available transport was mobilized and put in use. The first two armies that set off were the 49th and the 70th – their journey started on 4 and 5 April, respectively. They were followed on 6 April by Batov's 65th Army. The 2nd Shock Army was able to take the field only on 8 April. Part of the 19th Army also left on 5 April, but its main body was engaged in clearing the last German pockets of resistance and left by the middle of the month. The 5th Guards Tank Army, which was a tank army in name only, because it already had lost all its armor, was to remain in West Prussia as a security force.

While the troops were underway, Rokossovsky carried out on-the-spot inspections of the Oder front. He was accompanied by some members of his staff, as well as by the commanders of the 49th Army (Grishin) and 4th Air Army (Vershinin).

With all armies still in transit, Rokossovsky and his staff began careful planning of what was supposed to be the last Soviet offensive of the war. Following the Stavka instructions, they decided to deliver the main blow on the Front's left wing, on a 45-km frontage between Stettin and Schwedt, involving three armies (65th, 70th and 49th), three tank corps, a mechanized corps and a cavalry corps. Upon penetrating the enemy defense on the western bank of the West Oder, the "shock" group was to pursue the offensive in the general direction of Neustrelitz and between Day 12 and Day 15 was to reach the Demin – Wittenberge line.

After penetrating the enemy defense, each of the armies was to be reinforced with a tank corps (the 8th Mechanized Corps in the case of the 49th Army). The staff of the Front, however, had the last word on when the armored corps would be committed to battle. The 3rd Guards Cavalry Corps was to remain in the Front reserve and deployed behind the left flank of the 49th Army.

The artillery was to support the forced crossing of the Oder by the friendly infantry and penetrating the enemy main line of resistance. (In the main breakthrough sector a density of up to 150 tubes per kilometer was to be achieved.) Subsequently, it was to escort the forward rifle divisions and the formations exploiting the initial success.

On the eve of the offensive the 4th Air Army was to strike at German artillery positions, machinegun emplacements, headquarters and communication centers on the western bank of the West Oder. In the course of the offensive each of the three armies of the "shock" group would receive one air division of Il-2 Shturmoviks under operational control.

Much attention was also given to engineer support. Within shortest possible time the combat engineers brought up dozens of pontoons, hundreds of boats, as well as timber stocks for building bridges, landing stages, rafts, etc.

In the meantime the troops of the Front began to arrive. They gradually took over the positions of the friendly formations of the neighboring 1st Byelorussian Front (the 61st Army and the 1st Polish Army). On 13 April the forward units of Batov's 65th Army began to occupy the trenches along the Oder near Altdamm. The 70th Army of General Popov came up on 16 April; it was placed to the south, near Stettin. The positions on Rokossovsky's extreme left flank had been taken over on the previous day by Grishin's 49th Army. By 17 April the four armored corps of the Front also had completed their redeployment.

STRENGTH OF THE 2ND BYELORUSSIAN FRONT,
Beginning of April 1945

Personnel (combat units): 352,625 men
5,196 artillery pieces
3,418 mortars
887 rocket launchers
823 tanks and self-propelled guns
1,109 combat aircraft

STRENGTH OF THE MOBILE FORMATIONS OF THE 2ND BYELORUSSIAN FRONT,
19 April 1945

3rd Guards Cavalry Corps: 18,863 men, 16,917 horses, 100 artillery pieces, 153 mortars, 49 tanks, 30 self-propelled guns
1st Guards Tank Corps: 9,975 men, 35 artillery pieces, 81 mortars, 54 tanks, 24 self-propelled guns
3rd Guards Tank Corps: 11,410 men, 45 artillery pieces, 83 mortars, 71 tanks, 44 self-propelled guns
8th Guards Tank Corps: 9,325 men, 9 artillery pieces, 50 mortars, 42 tanks, 35 self-propelled guns
8th Mechanized Corps (w/ 66th Guards Self-Propelled Artillery Brigade): 12,892 men, 31 artillery pieces, 104 mortars, 125 tanks, 64 self-propelled guns

A Soviet SU-76M self-propelled gun of undisclosed unit of the 2nd Byelorussian Front lost in combat. West Pomerania, late April 1945. (TsAMO)

Manteuffel's forces were divided between four corps and were quite weak, actually: one (former) security division, one infantry division, two Volks-Grenadier divisions, two naval-infantry divisions, several training, fortress, police and reserve formations, Volkssturm battalions and a considerable number of independent units and battle groups of no real military value whatsoever. The artillery arm was based mostly on Flak-guns, while most of the AFVs were gathered in the three assault-gun brigades.

The main reserve of 3. Panzer-Army were two SS divisions of regimental strength (*"Langemarck"* and *"Wallonien"*). The 7. Panzer-Division also had begun to arrive, but after the catastrophe at the Gulf of Danzig, where it had lost nearly all of its equipment, it was yet to be rebuilt. (At that stage of the war any semblance of refurbishing was simply out of question; not surprisingly, the division received no tanks at all.)

The regular infantry formations still had some value, because each of them was formed around a core of battle-hardened veterans. The replacements that filled the ranks of the divisions were half-trained at best, but some of them were still highly motivated and therefore capable of putting up fanatical resistance. Heavy weapons were in short supply, but there was a considerable number of small arms, Panzerfausts and other types of light weaponry.

The defense of 3. Panzer-Army was strongest on the very sector where Rokossovsky intended to deliver his main attack, i.e. between Stettin and Schwedt. (In his memoir Rokossovsky admits that he was well aware of that, but "the circumstances" made it impossible to introduce any changes in the offensive plan approved by the Stavka.) It was up to 10 km in depth and comprised two to three defensive positions, each with

* * *

The 2nd Byelorussian Front was opposed by the forces of 3. Panzer-Army, which was led by one of the most experienced and highly decorated German officers, *General der Panzertruppe* Hasso von Manteuffel, a recipient of the Knight's Cross of the Iron Cross with Oak Leaves, Swords and Diamonds. That army was part of the order of battle of Army Group "Vistula" and was rather an infantry formation, because it had very few AFVs.

Marshal Rokossovsky awards soldiers of 2nd Byelorussian Front with medals for exceptional performance, June 1945. (RinP)

Marshal Rokossovsky on a horseback at the Victory Parade in Red Square, Moscow, 24 June 1945. (RinP)

one or two continuous lines of trenches. There were also foxholes and machinegun emplacements. Furthermore, all villages to a depth of 40 km from the Oder had been adapted for all-around defense and transformed into strongholds.

Like every other German late-war formation, the units of the 3. Panzer-Army were below their authorized strength. By 1 April the regular forces of the army totaled 69,637 men plus 3,258 auxiliaries, the so-called *Hiwi*. (These numbers didn't include the Luftwaffe, the Volkssturm, the SS, the foreign units, the Kriegsmarine, the field-training formations and so on.) The combat-effective strength at the disposal of Manteuffel was only 27,595.

AFV STRENGTH OF 3. PANZER-ARMY, 13 APRIL 1945

Anti-Tank Battalion 1: 4 StuG III, 12 StuG IV (11 operational), 5 Jagdpanzer 38(t) (4 operational)
281. Infantry-Division: 10 Jagdpanzer 38(t)
Assault-Gun Brigade 184: 24 StuG III (23 operational), 8 StuH 42
Panzer-Training Formation "Ostsee": 2 Pz V (1 operational), 4 Jagdpanzer IV (3 operational), 3 Jagdpanzer 38(t)
Anti-Tank Battalion 6: 19 Jagdpanzer 38(t) (17 operational)
Assault-Gun Brigade 210: 16 StuG III (15 operational), 14 StuH 42 (12 operational), 12 Pz IV/70 (11 operational)

THE LAST OFFENSIVE

The last offensive of the 1st Byelorussian Front was unleashed on the morning of 20 April. As usual, it was preceded by a powerful artillery preparation. Of the three formations of the "shock" group only Batov's 65th Army succeeded in securing a large bridgehead on the western bank of the Oder. Wasting no time, Batov ordered more troops to be ferried across. In the meantime the weather improved and this allowed the 4th Air Army to join the battle and to chase away the Kriegsmarine vessels shelling the assembly areas of the Soviet first echelon. At midday two 16-ton ferry crossings were already in operation. This allowed Batov to maintain the momentum of the offensive by moving additional forces to the western bank. By nightfall 31 rifle battalions with fifty 45-mm anti-tank guns, seventy mortars and fifteen SU-76M self-propelled guns already had been transferred to the foothold.

The Germans attempted immediately to eliminate the dangerous penetration and launched several resolute counterattacks of battalion strength accompanied by small groups of tanks and assault guns. They were beaten back with heavy losses by Batov's men.

The bridgehead quickly mushroomed and by the end of the day was already 6 km wide and 1.5 km in depth. After reviewing the situation Rokossovsky decided to take advantage of the success of the 65th Army and let the units of the 2nd Shock Army use one of Batov's crossings to move troops to the western bank with the objective of enveloping Stettin to the south and west. Further south the 70th Army also succeeded in securing a bridgehead. In contrast, the 49th Army was not able to achieve a success, mainly because its artillery preparation proved to be a total failure.

On 21 April the struggle for the bridgeheads continued with growing ferocity. The 49th Army finally succeeded in securing a small bridgeheads and the 70th Army also managed to advance a little bit further to the west. It became apparent that a breakthrough in the respective sectors of both armies was unlikely. Nevertheless, Rokossovsky decided that the 49th and 70th Armies had to continue their attacks in order to pin down as many German units as possible. At the same time, the main blow would be delivered by the 65th Army. For that purpose it was to receive additional reinforcements.

Field Marshal Bernard Law Montgomery, Marshal Zhukov and Marshal Rokossovsky meet at the Brandenburg Gate in Berlin, July 1945. (RinP)

* * *

By 25 April the 65th and 70th Armies had gained about 8 km of ground. Having beaten back several sharp German counterattacks, on 25 April the units of the 65th Army finally made a breach in Manteuffel's defensive line that was about 20 km wide. The German units facing the army had been decimated in the bloody fighting and Rokossovsky saw a wonderful opportunity to exploit that breach. The following ambitious objectives were assigned to the armies:

- The 65th Army, together with the 1st Guards Tank army, was to attack in the northwesterly direction and push the German troops operating to the north of the Stettin – Rostock line to the sea.
- The 2nd Shock Army was to attack with two rifle corps towards Stralsund, securing Rügen Island in the process.
- The 70th Army, with the 3rd Guards Tank Corps in the lead, was to advance toward Wismar.
- The 49th Army, reinforced with the 8th Mechanized Corps and the 3rd Guards Cavalry Corps, was to attack straight to the west and reach the Elbe.
- The 19th Army was to advance strictly along the seacoast and secure the port of Swinemünde at the mouth of the Oder.

On 26 April the assault groups of the 65th Army secured Stettin; Rokossovsky immediately relocated his HQ there. Then Batov's divisions, spearheaded by the 3rd Guards Tank Corps, rapidly advanced to the northwest.

On the next day the 2nd Shock Army reached Swinemünde and approached Stralsund. The unfortunate units of the former garrison of Stettin, which were desperately trying to avoid Soviet captivity, were intercepted and annihilated.

On 3 May the vanguard of the 3rd Guards Tank Corps reached Wismar, a town of a Hansa style on the Elbe, where contact with the British 2nd Army was finally established.

On 4 May the 70th and 49th Armies, as well as 8th Mechanized Corps and the 3rd Guards Cavalry Corps, also reached the Elbe on a broad front and got in touch with the Allies. The fighting along the Baltic coast continued for one more day. They cleared Rügen Island and islands in the mouth of the Oder.

On 9 May two divisions of the 19th Army landed on Bornhlm, a Danish island in the Baltic Sea, and seized it after a brief battle. The German garrison (about 12,000 strong, including some 1,200 wounded and ill) surrendered. This was the last military act of the 2nd Byelorussian Front in the World War II.

Rokossovsky (right) attends a session of the Sejm (the Polish parliament) in Warsaw, October-November 1956. (NAC)

Marshal Rokossovsky pictured in Moscow during the 22nd Congress of the Communist Party of the Soviet Union, October 1961. (RinP)

A portrait photo of Marshal Rokossovsky taken in 1960s. (RinP)

SOURCES

ARCHIVE MATERIAL

- Bundesarchiv-Militärarchiv, Freiburg: RH 2, RH 10.
- National Archives, Washington D.C.: Microfilmed records series T311, T312, T314.
- Tsentral'nyi Arkhiv Ministerstva Oborony [Central Archive of the Ministry of Defense of the
- Russian Federation], Podolsk: various funds.

PUBLISHED DOCUMENT COLLECTIONS

- Gryler A. N. et al. (Eds.). *Boevoi sostav Sovetskoi Armii.* Vol. 3 and 4. Moscow: Voenizdat, 1990.
- Zolotarev V. et al. (Eds.). *Velikaia Otechestvennaia Voina.* Vol. 16(5-4). Moscow: Terra, 1995 - 2001.

BOOKS

- Drabkin, Artem. (Ed.) *Panzer Killers.* Barnsley: Pen & Sword, 2013.
- Drabkin, Artem. (Ed.) *Ya dralsya s Panzerwaffe.* Moscow: Yauza-Eksmo, 2007.
- Duffy, Christopher. *Red storm on the Reich.* New York: Da Capo Press, 1993.
- Fey, Will. *Armor Battles of the Waffen SS 1943-45.* Winnipeg: J.J. Fedorowicz Publishing, 1996.
- Ganz, A. Harding. *Ghost Division.* Mechanicsburg: Stackpole Books, 2016.
- Glantz, David. (Ed.) *1985 Art of War Symposium.* Carlisle: US Army War College, 1985.
- Glantz, David M. and House, Jonathan. *When Titans Clashed.* Lawrence: University Press of Kansas, 1995.
- Grossman, Vasily. *A Writer at War.* London: The Harvill Press, 2005.
- Guderian, Heinz. *Panzer Leader.* London: Macdonald Futura Publishers, 1980.
- Klapdor, Ewald. *Viking Panzers.* Mechanicsburg: Stackpole Books, 2011.
- Meyer, Kurt. *Grenadiers.* Mechanicsburg: Stackpole Books, 2005.
- Rokossovsky, Konstantin. *A Soldier's Duty.* Moscow: Progress Publishers, 1985.
- Rokossovsky, Konstantin. *Soldatsky Dolg.* Moscow: Veche, 2013.
- Schäufler, Hans. *Knight's Cross Panzers.* Mechanicsburg: Stackpole Books, 2010.
- Schäufler, Hans. *Panzer Warfare on the Eastern Front.* Mechanicsburg: Stackpole Books, 2012.
- Shtemenko, Sergei. *The Last Six Months.* New York: Doubleday & Company, 1977.
- Werth, Alexander. *Russia at War 1941-1945.* New York: E. P. Dutton & Co, 1964.
- Wood, Ian Michael. *Tigers of the Death's Head.* Mechanicsburg: Stackpole Books, 2013.
- - . *Armored Bears.* Vol. 2. Mechanicsburg: Stackpole Books, 2013.
- - . *Istoria na Vtorata Svetovna Voina 1939 - 1945.* Vol. 8 and 9. Sofia: Voenno izdatelstvo, 1980.